REACH

REACH

40 BLACK MEN SPEAK ON LIVING, LEADING, AND SUCCEEDING

EDITED BY

Ben Jealous
and Trabian Shorters

Foreword by Russell Simmons

ATRIA PAPERBACK

NEW YORK LONDON TORONTO SYDNEY NEW DELHI

ATRIA PAPERBACK
A Division of Simon & Schuster, Inc.
1230 Avenue of the Americas
New York, NY 10020

Copyright © 2015 by BMe Networks, Inc.

First Atria Paperback edition February 2015

ATRIA PAPERBACK and colophon are trademarks of Simon & Schuster, Inc.

For information about special discounts for bulk purchases, please contact Simon & Schuster Special Sales at 1-866-506-1949 or business@simonandschuster.com.

The Simon & Schuster Speakers Bureau can bring authors to your live event. For more information or to book an event, contact the Simon & Schuster Speakers Bureau at 1-866-248-3049 or visit our website at www.simonspeakers.com.

Interior design by Kyoko Watanabe
Interior illustrations by Kwesi Ferebee, Design Action Collective

Manufactured in the United States of America

10 9 8 7 6 5 4 3 2 1

Library of Congress Cataloging-in-Publication Data is available.

ISBN 978-1-4767-9983-4
ISBN 978-1-4767-9985-8 (ebook)

BEN:
To my children, Jack and Morgan, and my nieces and
nephews Nina, Dylan, Emma, Tristan, and De'Juan.

TRABIAN:
To my grandfather Kennis Hutchons, whose
love made me want to honor men like him,
and to his wife, Irma Lee Hutchons, whose
love transformed my grandfather's life.

Special thanks go out to Nicole Levey,
Kweli Washington, and Ben Wrobel for their tireless
dedication and commitment to this project.

CONTENTS

REACH

FOREWORD

Russell Simmons

We lived for that loud, ghetto, b-boy hip-hop. For Run-DMC, that was our only real inspiration. We hated disco and R&B. We were rock 'n' roll from day one. When we made beats we would sample from artists like Billy Squier and Aerosmith. Sometimes it was jazz artists like Bob James who influenced us, but it was mainly rock 'n' roll. We were loud and abrasive, and rock 'n' roll had the beat. Most folks didn't see us as rock 'n' roll (shame on the gatekeepers), but progressive critics recognized our sound. From "Jam Master Jay" and "Sucker MCs" to *Raising Hell* and *Tougher Than Leather*, we were always hard, rebellious spirits.

The funny thing is that back then, black people didn't seem to like rap music. They rejected it at first. It was actually the white press that made us popular. The first time I heard my record on the radio was in Europe, in Amsterdam. In fact, if it wasn't for a white, British A&R director in 1979, who believed in our music, we may never have been able to take over the world.

✦

Although our style of music was first embraced by white audiences, don't think that I ever forgot what it's like to be a black man in America. No matter what industry I was breaking down the doors of, I was constantly reminded of the color of my skin. I still am. I'm aware that, for black men today, racism is still an obstacle that causes tremendous anger and suffering. Our communities are still recovering from years of soul-destroying policies and programs. And recently there have been undeniable roadblocks placed in our path toward greater freedom and prosperity. Whether it's the kind of racially charged violence that led to the deaths of Trayvon Martin, Mike Brown, Jordan Davis, and countless other black, unarmed young men; or the predatory mortgages that invaded our neighborhoods, which also helped bring our economy to the worst economic recession our generation has ever known; or the high unemployment rate that continues to devastate our communities; or the continuation of America's obsession with warehousing millions of us in prisons and jails across the country—our people have been hit hard.

There are times when it seems that we have been beat over the head with a baseball bat, over and over again. But, somehow, some way, we are able to get back up. We are able to stand back up on our own two feet and try again to climb to the top of the mountain. This has been the story of our people, the story of black people, the story of black men. This has been my story.

✦

Our ancestors survived the slave fields and somehow persevered. And they not only passed on these two necessary skills—survival and perseverance—to the generations of black

people that followed, they also taught us ingenuity. With very little they were able to continue living through brutal and harsh conditions. Since slavery, the conditions have certainly gotten better, but for many of us, we still struggle to survive. If I hadn't remembered the lessons of our ancestors during my own struggle, that essentially I could not fail until I quit, I know I would have not gotten to this point in my life. I definitely would not have been asked to write the foreword to this book from my dear friend Ben Jealous. I might not have even made it out of Hollis, Queens. I might have given up because I thought it would be too hard to overcome the obstacles in my path.

Instead, I'm reminded of a mantra that those who practice yoga constantly repeat: "Smile and breathe in every pose," no matter how difficult or painful the pose might be in that moment. No matter how great the challenge is, you must breathe deep and keep pushing through. That is what the great men in this book have done during the course of their lifetimes. That is what Ben Jealous has done. Never have any of us taken the easy route, as the easy route didn't even exist on our map.

✦

As I reflect back, I certainly could have let those who judged me by the color of my skin decide how my life would turn out. But instead I decided to challenge every norm that society had to offer. First I put rock 'n' roll on rap albums. Then I put the logos of black fashion designers on shirts worn by kids of all races all across the world. I made late-night HBO a place where great black comedians had the chance to make you laugh no matter the color of your skin. I created a financial services industry that provided access to the American Dream for millions of "unbanked" people in the United States. And finally, in my latest Hollywood adventure, I am uplifting talented folks in our

communities so that they get a fair shot at having their stories heard.

This is my rhythm—a loud drumbeat that contains a brighter outlook and a stronger purpose for us black men. A song we can all sing with a beat that raises hell and is always *tougher than leather*.

INTRODUCTION

Ben Jealous

I was blessed to grow up in a home where stories of great black men and women were served up as frequently as spoon bread and fried apples.

My grandmother told and retold stories of ancestors who had been born slaves and went on to found universities and banks and become statesmen during Reconstruction. My grandfather maintained an informal basement bar where I spent valuable evenings and weekend afternoons listening to his friends, all of whom were born into segregation but rose up above the walls of limitation. My parents told me bedtime tales about their experiences fighting Jim Crow with the Student Nonviolent Coordinating Committee (SNCC), the Congress of Racial Equality (CORE), and the National Association for the Advancement of Colored People (NAACP).

Together, these stories inspired me to dream big dreams of helping to increase opportunity for all people. Perhaps even more importantly, they instilled in me the habit of seeking out the stories of others. Their stories and the dreams they inspired started me on my own path toward leadership.

Since the beginning of time, imitation has always been the first step for those who achieve great things. Children pick up sticks to reenact the battles of great soldiers. Toddlers preach to congregations of teddy bears and puppets. Babies step into their parents' shoes and try to walk. However, here's the rub: each of us can only imitate what we know. We cannot imitate that which we have never seen, heard, or read about.

✦

Despite the rapid advances of technology, young men of color today often lack access to positive images and stories about others who look like them. With the exception of stories about one black man who lives at 1600 Pennsylvania Avenue, the reporting we see about men of color on the nightly news often leaves little good to imitate.

Occasionally, the images of our greatest heroes do break through. Black-and-white film reels of Martin Luther King Jr. and Thurgood Marshall flicker in classrooms on rainy days across the country. However, the grainy images place these icons in another era, in a time when the battles seemed perhaps simpler, the outcomes predetermined. Their lives are remembered in a way that makes them so flawless, so impossibly angelic, that their stories and achievements seem unattainable.

This is a book of everyday heroes. It is a collection of men known and unknown, most of whom have grown up since desegregation, all of whom have faced challenge, and all of whom have lived their lives in ways that are relevant to each of us. It is offered as a gift of gifts: each man featured in these pages sat down with us to tell his story so that it could be combined with the stories of others and handed down from parents, godparents, aunts and uncles, older brothers and peers to young men seeking to find their way.

My hope is that this book will empower you, as my family's

stories empowered me, with examples of black men who have overcome great challenges to do even greater things. I encourage you to read these stories, to ask your elders for their own and, ultimately, empowered with that new knowledge, to live a life of meaning that will leave a legacy for generations to come.

INTRODUCTION

Trabian Shorters

Y<small>ou</small> could hear a pin drop when I told my board of directors at the John S. and James L. Knight Foundation that I would step down in three months to build a new network called the BMe Community. The sudden hush was followed by raucous applause.

Through the course of my work at the Knight Foundation, I enjoyed incredible access to elite people and their information, and I stumbled upon a number of discoveries that made it imperative to launch BMe.

We are in the middle of the biggest cultural transfer in the history of the nation. The baby boomers, who have defined the American story for decades, are aging out at the exact moment that the millennial generation is coming of age. The millennials are inheriting the narrative left behind by these analog immigrants to their digital world, but they aren't necessarily embracing it.

On the contrary, America on the millennials' watch will no longer have a racial majority. All of the social myths will be updated, for better or for worse. If we make a concerted effort

to understand each other over the next decade, I think we can change them for the better.

This optimism is based, in part, on the social science that has permeated popular culture over the past few years—the research and writing of Daniel Kahneman, Chip and Dan Heath, and others. Our brains use all sorts of shortcuts to process information. People make decisions based not upon facts, but upon their *perceptions* of reality, and these perceptions are primed by the stories already running in our heads. As a result, we are prone to certain consistent, persistent mistakes in perception.

One of these mistakes is that "what you see is all there is." When black males are portrayed everywhere we look in a negative light, our brains—no matter our race or sex—are prone and primed to believe that this portrayal is correct, even the norm. In fact, it's not. Not by a long shot.

People, however, need more than just statistics to change their perspectives. Statistics are often rejected if they do not reinforce preexisting beliefs. On the other hand, *stories* involving relatable characters are "experienced" by the mind. When we hear a story, we put ourselves in that person's shoes for a minute. The story gives us an opportunity to reconsider our perspective and position. And we tend to choose the perspective that leaves us looking the best, even if that means discarding a mistaken position from before.

This is a book of stories about men whom you know but perhaps have not been perceiving fully. They are normal black men. They are good men. They are imperfect men, flawed, with struggles just like yours and decisions just as good or just as poor as some that you've made. Every one of the men in this book is also a community builder, somebody who wants us all to live in a more caring and prosperous world.

✦

We encourage everyone, of all races and sexes, to explore life through the eyes of these men. Once you do, it will become very easy to see brothers like these in your day-to-day life.

The mission of the BMe Community is to build caring and prosperous communities inspired by black men. All proceeds from the sale of this book will go to support that positive aspiration. Anyone can join the BMe Community, regardless of race or sex, because our mission is actually about building communities, not about saving the black man. We believe in building upon positive people, positive aspirations, and positive opportunities to tell the truth to one another and work together for a better future.

STORIES

D'Wayne Edwards

AGE: 45

TITLE: Founder of PENSOLE Footwear Design Academy

COMMUNITY: Inglewood, CA

There's a Bruce Lee quote that goes, "To hell with circumstances, I create opportunities." That's been a motto for me.

Ever since I was eleven years old, I knew I wanted to design footwear. I knew that before I even knew what a designer was or that you could make a career out of designing footwear. And believe me, there were a lot of doubters, a lot of people who said it couldn't happen. But they were wrong.

I grew up in Inglewood, California, right down the street from the Forum, where the Lakers played. Inglewood, at the time, was one of the roughest cities in America. I was the youngest of six kids. My mom raised us by herself. She was a bookkeeper at Centinela Hospital. She worked hard to ensure that we all had what we needed, even fighting through a severe back disability that caused her to undergo over fifteen surgeries until the last one took her life.

3

Two of my brothers, Ronnie and Michael, were blessed with artistic gifts. Both of them could draw beautifully. When I saw what they were doing, I wanted to do it too. I started out by taking what they'd drawn and trying to repeat it. Then I'd show it to them and they'd sit with me and show me the steps. They help me realize that I too had an artistic gift: I could really draw.

I was a good student in school and played sports, but my real passion was drawing. The Lakers used our high school gym as a practice facility—that was how the NBA was at the time—so we had close-up exposure to NBA players like Magic Johnson and Kareem. I loved to draw athletes. After I mastered the human body, I became fascinated with drawing the athletes' gear, inventing crazy designs for their shoes. I realized that there was limitless potential to make their footwear really complicated, really unique.

It was around that time that my older brother Michael died in a car accident. I was sixteen when he passed. It was a milestone moment for me; I knew I had to make something out of my life. He had really encouraged me to pay attention to my gift, and not waste it. After he died, I redoubled my resolve to design footwear as a profession.

✦

In high school, I didn't know anyone who worked as an artist or a designer. To me—and most of the people around me—artists were people you never really heard of until they were dead. And design? Didn't know what it was. When I told my high school guidance counselor that I wanted to create footwear for a living, she shook her head and said I was crazy. I remember taking that as motivation—it made me determined to figure out a way.

When I was a senior in high school, I entered a national sneaker design competition sponsored by Reebok. And I won.

The prize for winning the competition was a job, but Reebok couldn't even offer me a job since I was still in high school. Receiving that recognition and by such a large company was just the confidence booster I needed. Still, because I was the youngest of six siblings, there was no money for college, no money for design school upon graduation. So I had to figure out another way.

◆

The first real adult mentor I had was Robert Greenberg, the founder of the shoe company LA Gear. After I won the Reebok competition, Robert saw my potential. When I graduated from high school, he gave me a job at LA Gear as a file clerk. That was all I needed—I just needed to get in the door.

Failure was not an option. I was determined to prove that Robert had not made a mistake by bringing me in. I was determined to succeed in my role so the next person coming behind me who looked like me (and there were so few of us) could be given the chance as well.

At LA Gear's headquarters, there were suggestion boxes in every department so employees could submit ideas to make the company better. For the next six months, every day, I put a sketch of a new shoe design in that box. Each sketch also had a note suggesting that I be hired as a footwear designer. My persistence paid off, and after six months of trying, I was hired to work in the design department.

A few years later, I followed Robert to Skechers, where he gave me another big shot: the chance to head up the design department. Remember, at this time there were only *three* other Black designers in the entire footwear industry. This was rarefied air.

◆

After several years at Skechers I was recruited by Nike, and then in 2000 Michael Jordan recruited me to come work for his brand. Working with him was a powerful experience. I had grown up drawing my own versions of the Air Jordan, but I never could have imagined that I'd have the chance to work for Jordan himself.

I remember when I was given the nod to design the twenty-first and twenty-second editions of the Air Jordan shoe. It was truly a rare opportunity—only five people had ever done it before me.

It was a dream come true, but the opportunity also posed a challenge: people didn't really care about the twenty-first and twenty-second editions. The twentieth edition was big because that was a major milestone. The twenty-third edition was expected to be the last; the collection would finish with the number Jordan made famous. So I had to do something that made my editions really pop.

I did some research on the number 22 and discovered that there was a stealth fighter jet that had used the number. I got inspired by the concept of "stealth," as in, these editions of the Air Jordan sneaker were going to sneak up on people. I began to work out this concept of stealth, the art of deception, creating an illusion that masks mastery.

I presented the concept to Michael Jordan, and the first thing I asked him was how and when he became "stealth." How did he master his craft and how did he disguise his genius from people so he could exploit their weaknesses? I wish I had had a tape recorder. He talked about how when he was dialed in, everything around him slowed down. When he was on the court, he was the only person moving full speed; everyone else was moving in slow motion. This ability helped him anticipate what others would do before they did it.

Michael's message really boiled down to living and playing

in the present. And I've translated that approach to how I design and how I exist, how I live my life. The Jordan 22s were a success—they generated $100 million in sales.

◆

In 2007 I started having a conversation with Nike about the future of design talent. I explained to them that I didn't enter design in the traditional way—like a lot of kids from my background, I didn't even know what design school was. So I proposed a design competition to level the playing field.

Up to that point, Nike recruited designers from colleges. I said to them, what would happen if you invested in kids at an earlier age? I looked at the competition as an opportunity to do the same sort of talent search that the Nike marketing department does to find the next great high school basketball player. Rather than scouring gyms for people showing promise in running and dunking, we would do a nationwide design competition and find the kids who love sketching and doodling and don't know they can actually build a career out of it. I called the competition Future Sole, and Nike agreed to sponsor it.

The Future Sole competition had a successful four years, including endorsements by Lisa Leslie and Carmelo Anthony. The competition proved that there was so much young talent out there. It motivated me to follow through with an idea I'd had for years to create a school for young designers, and to help bring more diverse talent into the footwear industry. I named it the PENSOLE Footwear Design Academy—a tribute to the #2 pencil I've always used for design, and the product that our students create.

Footwear in the United States is a $50 billion industry. Black Americans in particular spend a huge amount of money on sneakers. We are the largest consumer of the product.

Sneakers have become a significant part of Black American culture and style. So much so that we hit a point where we started to kill each other over the product. Sneakers became more important than somebody's life? Sneakers became more important than paying your bill? Sneakers became more important than opening a checking or savings account?

My goal with the PENSOLE Academy is to show kids that we can do more than have that lust and desire for a sneaker; we can also make a really good living off of it. We can stop being consumers and become contributors. Our path is not limited only to wearing the sneakers and playing sports—we can also be involved in so many other aspects of the business, like design or marketing.

My theory is that young people respond to what they are exposed to. If all they see are athletes, that's the path they believe is available to them. That was the case for a lot of my high school classmates—we'd see the Lakers on campus and we would idolize them.

On the other hand, if young people see me and I'm telling them about the career I've built designing footwear, it opens up new realms. If they learn about marketing, sales, finance, and the other functions that support the production, distribution, and sale of footwear, their options are expanded even further. It allows them to say, "I'm a great communicator. Why don't I study communications in college and then get a job in sales where my talents and skills can be deployed productively, where I can build a career?"

I'm proud of how far PENSOLE has come. At this point I have mentored more than fifty Black designers currently working in the industry. We have created a robust pipeline of talent that is getting the guidance and support they need to make an impact in the industry down the road.

We're helping young people build their confidence, helping

them understand that they are capable of mastering their craft, of transcending their circumstances and creating their own opportunities. We want them to understand that they are stealth, like Michael Jordan—that they have the power to slow down the environment around them so they can navigate through it for maximum success and realize their true potential.

Rashaun Williams

AGE: 20

TITLE: Cofounder and President/CEO, Phresh Philly; DJ; Director of Youth and Millennial Initiatives, Techbook Online; BMe Leader

COMMUNITY: Philadelphia, PA

I'm a DJ. I'm an environmentalist and a social entrepreneur. I'm a business owner. I'm a mentor. I'm an artist. I'm twenty years old. I'm black. I'm committed to changing my community.

I'm from Philadelphia; born and raised all over Germantown. My mom and dad separated before I could walk, but I've had very loving and fulfilling relationships with both my parents. I'd spend weekdays with my mom and grandmother and some weekends with my father, and even though they both struggled with the personal and professional dimensions of poverty, nothing ever stopped them from giving me unconditional love. We may have had to ration our meals until the next paycheck, but we never went hungry, always leaving home with a healthy breakfast and lunch to carry us through the day.

One specific and lasting memory I have was moving a lot

when I was growing up. I recently counted fifteen moves. That constant transience numbed me a bit, giving me a sense that nothing in life was permanent.

By the time I reached middle school, I was a master communicator and very actively involved in extracurricular activities. Since I was already a geek, already a nerd, already deeply involved in fifth-grade student council, middle school would just be time to take everything to another level. Whenever there was an opportunity to get more involved in my school community, I was there. If there was an opportunity to volunteer, take an art class, represent the student government, take part in poetry and oratory contests, join the drum squad, or pick up violin lessons, I was there.

By eighth grade, I was the president of the Student Council, and as I continued to bring an unbridled natural energy to anything I did, it seemed as though my school's staff members and other students began to respond positively to that.

◆

When I was in middle school I began to really form my identity in Philadelphia's teen "party scene." I was still finding myself, still involved in extracurricular activities, but I started to party a lot as well. Newly introduced to the nightlife, I always celebrated with my right-hand man Troy, one of my best friends to this day. Our bikes were our cars—we would ride our bikes all around the neighborhood to meet with family members and friends almost every day of the week in the summertime—but it was probably our mutual love for music that made us brothers, fostering and inspiring the DJ inside of me.

I remember walking into a club the first time: the DJ was phenomenal, leaving no room for inertia on the dance floor, making the overall experience truly amazing. Though it may be perceived negatively, partying was never a negative thing for

me. Music gave people in my neighborhood and beyond the opportunity to meet, listen to new music, make new friends, and build new memories. To be a part of that experience was one of the most positive things to ever happen in my life.

By the time I hit high school, I was deep into music and healthy living. I was also kicking ass in terms of my grades and extracurriculars. With experience producing music both live and electronically before, I began to make beats. Eventually with the merger of me making music in my spare time and my love of parties, people said I should DJ, and by tenth grade, it was official.

With a couple of parties under my belt, I participated in a weeklong entrepreneurship camp at the Enterprise Center in West Philadelphia. There were about four hundred kids in the program, and I was among the youngest, probably one or two grades below the other participants. We had a competition for the best entrepreneur based on presentation, understanding of demographics, and marketing, and the winner got $500 to start his or her business. I won the competition by pitching an idea to make customized items like sneakers. I used my awarded $500 to purchase a turntable simulator. I was setting myself up to become a DJ professionally.

Over time, DJ'ing took me all over Philly and places outside of Philly. It became my business, and it led me to experience other people's cultures. I DJ'd for families from Pakistan, Latino families, Jamaican families. It gave me a deeper appreciation for the collective challenges we face in Philadelphia and beyond.

✦

I mentioned healthy living, and that is another real passion of mine; something that I've been able to tie in with my love of music and my love of the people in my city.

Many black people in communities of poverty go to the

corner store to buy Doritos, Hugs (which are sugary drinks), Twizzlers, and that sort of thing. That was breakfast for so many kids in my high school and around my neighborhood. That's not even really food. It's just sucrose. It's the type of thing that gives you a sugar rush and then you crash.

I was fortunate in that my mom imposed a structure at home wherein I always started the day with a healthy breakfast. That made me a very conscious eater—I became a vegetarian in the eleventh grade—and it was one of the best decisions I've made in my life.

Looking back at my earlier years, I know that every young person I shared a classroom with was just as sociable, artistic, and effective at communicating as me. But they didn't end up with the same opportunities. One reason is that they were starting from a deficit if they didn't have access to healthy food. When it comes to junk food, I've internalized the difference between "brain food" and "attention deficit disorder food." It's hard to contemplate being attentive, being creative, and making social and economic progress if our young people are starting from such a deficit with respect to their personal health and nutrition.

✦

My work has woven together DJing, advancing healthy living, and improving the environment in which we live through social entrepreneurship. I started an organization with two friends, Douglas Wallace and Anthony Torrance, called Phresh Philly.

Essentially, Phresh Philly started as a vehicle for community organizing with a special emphasis on high school volunteerism and social entrepreneurship. Our goal was to literally clean up Philly. Philly consistently ranks as one of the dirtiest cities in America, while Pennsylvania is the eleventh most polluted

state in the nation. I knew all this stuff because I could see it every day as I walked through the neighborhood. As my friends and I witnessed the over sixty thousand vacant houses in the city, we wanted to improve the quality of living. It struck me that if we could get people to care about their neighborhoods, about cleaning up communities, we could kick-start real value creation.

We started Phresh Philly while still in high school, doing small initiatives: community cleanups, cookouts, and other things that improved our "hood." With the help of some of my mentors, we secured funding and support from other organizations around Philly. We came up with creative ways to get young people engaged. On any given day, we'd bring out thirty to fifty kids from our school and other schools to volunteer around the neighborhood, helping to get the word out about environmental sustainability and participating in services to improve the environment directly.

When I spoke to kids and adults in the neighborhood, it was clear to me that we really needed to promote entrepreneurship as well. Since then, Phresh Philly has evolved so that we're training young people in social entrepreneurship so they can create their own opportunities that serve the global community.

◆

In the end, I believe that everybody really wants the same things: safety, health, wealth, and love. When I summarize my life to date, I put it in these terms: music, mentorship, and motivation. These, I believe, are important underpinnings to the work that I do and critical pieces in ensuring that black males, and indeed all human beings, are genuine assets to their communities.

After high school I attended Temple University. In the fall of my sophomore year, people asked me how my summer

went and I told them about the successes we had achieved with Phresh Philly. After I got finished telling them, they all said, "Well, it seems like you've got it figured out already." Eventually, I believed that statement for myself and stopped going to school so I could take more time to work on my social entrepreneurial goals. Since then, I've been a full-time entrepreneur working every day to build communities, mentor young people, save the environment. Taking this leap is the best professional decision I've made in my life.

Whenever I'm asked about what other young people should decide to do about college, I always tell young people to imagine their future and determine for themselves what the best vehicles are to get there. Get a degree in your dreams, graduate from your goals, create your career, and love the life that you've learned to live.

I'm often reminded of a Native American proverb that says "we don't inherit the land from our ancestors, we borrow it from our grandchildren." In a nutshell, that's what my life is all about—empowering young people to build their futures and live environmentally sustainable lives here in Philadelphia, and the rest of the planet.

John Legend

AGE: 36

TITLE: Musician and Philanthropist

COMMUNITY: New York, NY

When I was young and my parents took us to the library, I was always attracted to stories about civil rights leaders and abolitionists, the great leaders who made huge social change happen. One of the key themes that connect all those people's lives is that they dedicated themselves unconditionally to their cause, to approaching their work with love and a willingness to sacrifice. Like them, when I signed my first record deal with Sony, I knew I wanted to find a way to give back, to put my success into the service of something bigger.

I was raised in Springfield, Ohio. My dad, Ron Stephens, worked on the assembly line at Navistar, a large truck manufacturer, for thirty years. My mother was a part-time seamstress and never worked outside of the home.

I grew up in my maternal grandfather's church. He was the pastor, my grandmother was the church organist, my mother

was the choir director. My father was a Sunday school teacher and a drummer, and he sang in the choir as well. When my grandfather retired, his son—my uncle—took over as pastor. So I was, in some part, raised by my extended family in addition to my mother and father.

My maternal grandmother was particularly influential for me musically. She taught me gospel music when I was young. Her musical style greatly impacted much of my early development as a pianist.

✦

When I wasn't singing or playing the piano, I was being homeschooled along with my siblings by my mother. As Pentecostals, my parents wanted us to have a Christian education. We'd started out in a private Christian school. However, over time, we couldn't afford the tuition. My parents opted to teach us from home with advisors from the private school as support.

Homeschooling was an important aspect of my upbringing. I was a voracious reader and learner, and so the independent study model played to my strengths. I could dive in deeply and forge ahead. The experience of being homeschooled provided me with a strong educational foundation that I might not have gotten if I had gone to a traditional public school.

✦

At age ten, when my maternal grandmother passed away, I don't think I'd ever been so sad. Understandably, my mother really struggled with the loss of her mom. She became depressed and had a very difficult time coping. Things were not the same for my family following the death of my grandmother. My parents decided to divorce when I was eleven years old.

My father took full custody of my two brothers, my sister, and me. As the most present male figure in my life, he's been

hugely influential to me: my outlook on life, the way I treat people, how I carry myself. My father is a very gentle soul and is even-keeled, not terribly emotional. I think I'm similar to him in a lot of ways.

There have been other role models and mentors too who've helped shape me, helped me set my goals and pursue them. My mother's brother, Uncle Raymond Lloyd, played a key role. He took over the church when my grandfather retired. He would take us to the gym every week, and we'd spend the night at his house a lot. Having both him and my father in my life was really positive because they were responsible, caring gentlemen who exhibited the character traits I wanted to embody as I grew older.

A lot of their teachings were biblically based, but the characteristics they promoted were things you'd want to promote no matter what your religious leanings. They emphasized being a gentleman, being humble, being giving, being considerate of others. As I think about it, this emphasis on character was a big part of how my extended family operated. We talked a lot about, and did our best to live up to, concepts of good character.

There were two other male figures who helped me along, especially during my high school years. One was Michael Dixon, my guidance counselor. He was one of the few black men on staff at my school. Mr. Dixon set me a very high bar and held me to it. He saw my potential and wanted to make sure that I didn't mess it up. It's important for a young person—even a self-motivated young person—to have that sort of guidance and support. Mr. Dixon was someone I was accountable to at school, someone whom I trusted and knew had my back.

Another key figure was Arlin Tolliver, the director of the community choir in our town. I started developing a reputation as one of the kids in town who could really sing. Arlin invited me to join the choir, which I participated in for several years. Like Mr. Dixon, Arlin pushed me a bit, held me accountable,

knew what to do to ensure I wouldn't let things slide. He saw my potential and wanted to help me maximize it. So he would get me a lot of gigs as a singer and pianist on the local church circuit, playing concerts, weddings, and funerals.

✦

After high school I attended the University of Pennsylvania. In addition to providing me with a phenomenal education experience, the decision to go to Penn had a profound impact on my music career. I didn't specifically know it when I decided to attend the school, but Philadelphia was a great place to be in the mid-1990s as a young musician.

The Roots and their crew were very active; they fostered a real flourishing of great music coming out of the city. Anytime they hosted an open mike, I'd go there and watch and try to perform. There were so many great artists who were either from Philly or who spent quality time there: Erykah Badu, Common, Musiq Soulchild, Bilal, the Roots. I didn't work with any of them at the time, but their presence provided me so much inspiration, it gave me a model as an artist when I was able to do my own thing. I met two of my musical collaborators, Dave Tozer and DeVon Harris (aka Devo Springsteen), while I was in Philly. DeVon is cousins with Kanye West, and so I met Kanye through DeVon. It's hard to say what would or would not have happened had I not gone to Penn, but it's safe to say that going to Penn put me around people who could help me move forward as a musician.

✦

When I say move forward, I should be clear that my music career didn't take off immediately. Even though I was passionate about music, I believed that I should not seal off other options that were available to me. If music didn't work out, I wanted to

have other choices in life. My education gave me options. As I was pursuing my music, I worked at jobs that offered great career paths as well. I started my career at the Boston Consulting Group (BCG), providing analysis and strategic guidance to Fortune 500 companies. I also worked at Management Leadership for Tomorrow (MLT), a diverse talent leadership development organization whose board I now sit on. I had a reputation among my colleagues for delivering on what I said I would do. So my approach was never about "forget school" or "I don't care about the job I'm working in." It was about a commitment to excellence in whatever I was doing. If I didn't get a record deal, I would still be okay.

I worked for the BCG and MLT for several years while performing at small gigs around New York City and showcasing my music to record labels. There were a lot of nos before there were any yeses, but I was committed to break through with music, something that I love, something that I believe brings goodness to the world. Through perseverance, luck, and help from friends like Kanye West who saw my talent and vouched for me, I was able to secure a major label deal with Sony in 2004. It was a dream come true, but I knew then that it was just the start of the journey, not the culmination of it.

✦

Nowadays, I compose, write, and record music, perform at concerts around the world, and work in television and movies.

When I was growing up, I wrote an essay in which I said I wanted to become a musician and then use my talents to help advance the causes like civil rights that I'd found inspiring as a young person. When I finally signed my first record deal with Sony, I started to look for ways to give back, to put my success into the service of something bigger.

✦

I started the Show Me Campaign as a vehicle for giving back. Our efforts began with supporting Jeffrey Sachs and Millennium Promise in the challenge of ending extreme poverty. I was able to see how Jeffrey and other philanthropists, like Bill Gates, are doing substantial work to support communities and make real progress on challenges that a lot of people thought were intractable. It made me want to get more involved.

I visited Ghana with Millennium Promise. I met a young girl named Rose. Seeing how Rose's family and others in their community were so committed to improving life for their kids was inspiring to me. We got involved in their community, and we've seen real improvement in health outcomes associated with malaria reduction, access to clean water, access to neonatal health, greater access to information. We've built schools and extended the opportunity for young girls like Rose to get scholarships to secondary schools when traditionally only their male counterparts did. The Show Me Campaign works with Millennium Promise to this day.

I was also inspired when I started visiting schools in New York City that were having dramatically higher success rates than other schools in the same communities. Visiting Harlem Village Academies and schools linked to the Harlem Children's Zone, Teach for America, and Turnaround for Children, among others, made me realize that in the right circumstances, the right environment, we can really create situations in which our kids can have much better educational outcomes than they do now. I came to see that the problems that many people thought were intractable and unsolvable could be addressed with the right efforts.

So many problems in education are interrelated. It's important that we fix our schools, have great teachers, great learning

resources, and really hold kids accountable for their success. But it's also important that we reform our criminal justice system so that our kids aren't growing up without fathers. It's important that we provide a stronger safety net so kids aren't going to school hungry and without health care.

I've chosen to focus on improving schools because that's an area that provides a lot of leverage. But the truth is, none of these things is independent. We have to hold our society accountable for addressing these challenges in combination, and that's why it is so important that we have a democracy that reflects people's interest and will, particularly those who are less well off.

Through music, I'm able to contribute to the betterment of the world—by giving people an important sound track to their lives, and by using my gifts to help other people through civic engagement.

When I reflect back, there was nothing more important to the outcome of my life than the early support I had from family and mentors outside of my home, the access to a piano to practice on, and forums like the church and the community choir in which to hone my craft. If I hadn't had all of those opportunities, who knows if I would be where I am now. And if I didn't have a solid grounding in those heroes from the civil rights movement and those in my family and in my community, I might not have the tools and the inspiration to apply my good fortune to causes that are attempting to make the world a better place.

Louis Gossett Jr.

AGE: 78

TITLE: Actor; Activist; Founder, Eracism Foundation

COMMUNITY: Brooklyn, NY; Malibu, CA

I am a stage, film, and television actor. I've been in the business for sixty years, having worked with some of the greatest artists of the twentieth century, white and black. Having come of age in the 1960s, I've also been deeply involved with political and social causes. At seventy-eight, I'm an elder statesman now. My main vocation is to communicate with younger generations— not just of actors, but of people—to transmit the values of community, self-love, and purpose that have characterized our progress as a people.

I was born and raised in Sheepshead Bay, Brooklyn, in 1936. We were the first generation of my family born out of the South, and we were an instrumental part of the exodus north to the "Promised Land."

Sheepshead Bay was primarily an Italian and Jewish neighborhood at the time, peppered with victory gardens for World

War II and flanked by fishing boats bobbing in the harbor. My father worked at a newsstand in Coney Island and later as janitor at the Brooklyn Borough Gas Company. He was also a first mate on a fishing boat. My mother was a domestic for three or four wealthier Irish, Italian, and Jewish families in our neighborhood. She took care of their children, so she had a special place of reverence in their communities. I grew up with the children. I was their friend and their schoolmate.

My great-grandmother had a home near ours. She couldn't read or write, yet she was the matriarch—the glue in the family. We believe that she was born a slave, and by our crude calculation she was 115 years old by the time she passed away. She took care of all of the grandkids while the parents were out working as maids, chauffeurs, and butlers.

My grandmother saw to it that we contributed for the good of our family and community—that we were responsible for ourselves and to each other. When we were old enough to carry water or weed a garden or gather eggs, we were expected to do so. When we headed out to school, she expected us to be dressed well, have our hair combed, and speak and behave in a manner that was respectable.

These were the tactics we deployed as a community that had come up from slavery, which wasn't that far in the rearview mirror.

✦

My male heroes as a child were my father and my uncles. I admired them for their athleticism, their charisma, their confidence, their stylish zoot suits, their command of the Lindy Hop and the Boogie Woogie.

All four of my uncles fought in World War II, and they returned from the battlefront broken men. When they returned home, I'd still see them exhibiting the attributes that I

respected, but I also noticed a sadness creeping in. The family gatherings on Friday evenings would have more drinking than cheer; the music and mood could turn somber, and fighting between family members grew more frequent.

It was the women—my great-grandmother, grandmother, mother, and my aunts—who were the breadwinners and who held the family together. When they got home from the war, the men didn't feel like men because they had to rely on their wives to take care of everything. They struggled to find their place in the working world and the family structure. None of them lived past sixty. Some didn't make it to fifty.

My other male heroes were Superman, Tarzan, Hopalong Cassidy, and Captain Marvel. They were all white. As a young kid, I remember looking at myself in the mirror, and it bothered me that I didn't look like Superman. I wanted to be like my heroes.

I remember lamenting to one of my white friends, Stanley Ralph Ross, that I loved Superman but I couldn't play him because I was black and he was white. Stanley immediately responded that being black wasn't an impediment to being Superman. "It don't bother what you look like, you're going to play Superman today." Yes, I could play him after all.

Stanley's matter-of-fact response became ingrained in my soul, and in a way, it became a metaphor for my years through the end of high school and into my career. From then on, I didn't feel a burden or a limitation from being black. It was the people I grew up with—my family, my teachers, the community—who gave me that liberty and that freedom.

✦

I felt that sense of opportunity in high school, where I was student body president and a decorated athlete. I was popular and respected in school, and in 1953, when I was a high school

senior, my teachers recommended to their producer friends that I debut in a new Broadway show at the Lyceum Theatre in Manhattan called *Take a Giant Step*.

This opportunity literally catapulted me forward a giant step. All of a sudden I was performing in a show with leading actresses like Estelle Hemsley, Estelle Evans, and Jane White. I was working with actors like Mr. Frederick O'Neal, the first African American to run Actors' Equity, who helped found the American Negro Theatre, where Harry Belafonte, Sidney Poitier, Ossie Davis, and Ruby Dee first cut their teeth.

My world began expanding. Backstage I got handshakes and hugs from the people who made our history. I was meeting the likes of Adam Clayton Powell and his wife, Hazel Scott, Mr. and Mrs. Ralph Bunche, Billie Holiday, Josephine Baker, and Paul Robeson.

These new experiences introduced a new duality, a tug-of-war, into my life. The world I grew up with and this new world had subtly different mores. The men and women I started to meet were so different from the people I grew up with. They were not killing themselves with alcohol and violence and low self-esteem. They were very responsible. They were pushing forward.

I loved the men in my family. I still wanted to be like them because they were great athletes. I still wanted to spend time with them. I understood that my success, my very access to this new world, was predicated on how far my family had come from the South—from the residue of slavery, from their destructive experiences in World War II, from their working-class struggles. But it was becoming more difficult to balance the two worlds.

✦

My film career soon took off, and at nineteen, I was offered a role in *The Bushbaby*, which was being filmed on location in

Nairobi, Kenya, and Tanzania, at the foot of Mount Kiliman-jaro. This opportunity to visit Africa helped me to broaden my sense of who my predecessors were. All of a sudden my list of heroes included not just Superman and Tarzan but also Jomo Kenyatta, who led Kenya into independence, and Kwame Nk-rumah, who oversaw Ghana's independence from Britain.

I was inspired by the Ashanti, Zulu, and Masai civilizations, and all the African kings who reigned before the first colonists came to Africa. They were successful for centuries before the Europeans got there. Their bottom-line rule was that every-thing one does must be done for the benefit of the whole. I recognized this rule as the same one I had learned from my great-grandmother, and I believed that it might just hold one of the answers for the salvation of mankind.

Back in New York, TV and film roles came to me, and I did my part to hone my craft. I joined the Actors Studio and worked with Marlon Brando, Marilyn Monroe, Paul Newman, Anthony Quinn, and James Dean. I filmed the TV movie *Companions in Nightmare*, and my career grew from there.

This was the 1950s and 1960s, and working in New York, I was part of a renaissance in music, culture, and politics—one that spawned Carole King, Richie Havens, Jackie Robinson, Bob Dylan, Woodstock, and so much more. It spread out of New York City and changed the morals and music of the entire country.

After a few years, the William Morris Agency, Lew Wasser-man, and others took me on their shoulders and brought me to Los Angeles. The first time I experienced outright racism was on my second trip to LA, when the agency flew me into town for *Companions in Nightmare*. They had booked me a room in the Beverly Hills Hotel and even rented me a convertible. The trip from the airport to the hotel should have taken thirty minutes, but on the way there I was stopped five or six times

by police officers. I was driving with the top down, listening to Sam Cooke, and clearly they thought I was in the wrong neighborhood.

Later that evening, I was walking around Beverly Hills, visiting movie stars' homes. A police officer approached me and asked what I was doing. When I told him, he arrested me for walking around at night, which was a discretionary measure that he did not have to take. He handcuffed me to a palm tree, and he had me hugging that tree for three hours. That day was the first episode of abject racism in my entire life.

Out in Los Angeles I did *Roots*, which allowed me an opportunity to act out the experiences of my ancestors. I played Sheriff Gilmore in *Lawman Without a Gun*, about the first black sheriff in Mississippi. I played Sergeant Emil Foley in *An Officer and a Gentleman*, for which I won the Academy Award for Best Supporting Actor. I was only the second African-American man to win an Academy Award in a supporting role.

◆

I am here today because of what I learned from my grandmother, my uncles, my father and mother, my teachers in high school, Dr. Martin Luther King, Nelson Mandela, my mentors in the entertainment industry, the crowds who celebrated me in Nairobi, and so many others who have shaped me into the man that I am today. I'm here to do whatever I can as an elder, as a "Baba," to the next generation.

I have two sons. One is named Satie Bertrand, after the French composer Eric Satie and Bertrand Russell. The other, named Sharron, I welcomed into my home when he was homeless at the age of six. Satie is a film director. Sharron is a chef.

I have humbly started a foundation called Eracism, and through the foundation we are trying to build the first Shamba Center in Inglewood, California. Shamba is a Swahili word

meaning "farm." I want to put in place the lessons I have learned in my life, so that we can all walk with pride like I did when I first went to Africa.

Through the Shamba Center, we're teaching an approach of "Back to Basics"—the basics that my grandmother imparted to my cousins and me when we were in her care: collective responsibility; empathy; being ready, willing, and able to help another person when he or she is down. This is really the basis of survival. One of the things I hope to do with the Shamba Center is to take young American gangbangers and fly them to a number of African countries, so they can experience what I experienced. I believe that when they come home, the trip will have eliminated some of the gangbanger mentality.

Many black males today don't have a sense of responsibility, a sense of direction, of possibility or opportunity. They have not been taught anything in this regard. They're wanting for instruction, and wanting for attention. And when they're neglected, they take matters into their own hands.

I believe that we can reverse this cycle. We can reverse it by teaching our young men that they come from rich traditions in Africa—that they are the descendants of kings and great inventors. They have great worth and their lives are worthy. We need to turn them from gangbangers into "Ambassadors of Peace." This sense of responsibility should be their foundation.

✦

I met Nelson Mandela when he emerged from prison after twenty-seven years. Everyone wondered what he would say. His message was simple: We have no time to focus on revenge, because it is a self-inflicting disease. The only thing we have time for is the uplifting of ourselves and one another for the bigger picture, which is the salvation of the planet.

We need to remember that bigger picture. Through the

Shamba Center, I hope to teach these children that when they grow up to be mothers and fathers, lawyers, police officers, doctors, and congresspeople, they will talk about the bigger picture. I hope that instead of talking about the salvation of the Irish or the Jew or the Black, they talk about the salvation of mankind, and of the planet. I think we can ask for and expect nothing less.

Shaka Senghor

AGE: 42

TITLE: National Outreach Rep for BMe;
Director of Atonement Project at
University of Michigan; BMe Leader

COMMUNITY: Detroit, MI

When I was sixteen I caught a case and ended up in a youth home. There was a girl I was seeing prior to getting locked up, and when I went away, she moved on to someone else. When I got out, she tried to reconnect with me—even though I knew she was with somebody else. So we got into an argument about it, and she ended up calling her boyfriend.

I remember I was standing around on the corner with one of my partners when the boyfriend rolled up, like, "What's up?" We exchanged words, and I thought he wanted to fight. But instead of getting out of the car to fight, he started shooting. The first two hit me in my leg, and I just remember running, thinking I didn't want to be shot in the back of my head. I was lucky that he only managed to shoot me again in the foot before I got away.

I was bleeding profusely, waiting for the ambulance as long

as I could—you know, in the 'hood, we have no expectations of the ambulance coming. I remember this feeling of vulnerability and never wanting to have this happen again.

I didn't like feeling vulnerable. I didn't like feeling like somebody could kill me over relatively nothing. So when I came out of the hospital, limping on crutches, I was super-defiant. The first thing I did? I bought a pistol and started carrying it with me every day. I made up my mind at that point that if I ever got into a conflict, I would shoot first.

A little over a year later I did get into another conflict, over a drug transaction gone wrong. I refused to sell to a guy I didn't know . . . it got out of hand . . . we exchanged words, and I shot first. I tragically caused his death. I was sentenced to seventeen to forty years in prison.

You would think that's the end of the story in most cases, but it's not. It marked the beginning of a long journey—one that I could not have possibly imagined at that time. My life has been like that, unpredictable in both bad ways and amazingly good ways.

I grew up on the east side of Detroit in the 1970s. Most of my days in the neighborhood were spent playing and eating fruit from the trees in different backyards. I was a happy child for the most part.

At a certain point my parents started having marital issues, and I started changing. I became less focused in school. I started running away from home, staying with whatever friends would have me.

This was right when crack was being introduced in Detroit. I got sucked into the crack culture. I was exposed to probably every horrific thing you can imagine in that environment: I was robbed at gunpoint by some addicts; one of my childhood friends was murdered in front of a crack house; I became addicted to smoking lace joints, which were crack-laced weed.

By the time I left the neighborhood to serve my time at age nineteen, I was a very different person from the young boy who grew up eating fruit from the trees.

✦

When I first got to prison, I vowed I would not leave the way I came in. And not necessarily in a good way.

I told myself, I'm going to leave more skilled at hustling, more callous and coldhearted in terms of how I would take over my community at home. For the majority of the rest of my sentence I was in either maximum security or close custody. Most of the guys with me were serving ten to a hundred years in prison. I ran a store inside the prison and had guys who worked for me and guys who feared me. I was on course to become the best predator I could be—if I ever got out.

That all changed in October 1999, when I received a letter from my son.

I was in solitary confinement, where I spent nearly five years of my incarceration. Solitary is dehumanizing. It's degrading. You're in your cell twenty-three hours a day, five days a week, and twenty-four hours a day two days a week. Each time you come out they put on handcuffs that are attached to a dog leash. When you go take a shower it's just a cage. It makes you start detaching yourself from your own body. But it was in this environment that I had the real breakthrough.

I was sitting in my cell in solitary when the guard handed me a letter from my son. He wrote, "Dad, Mom told me why you're in prison."

Reading this letter was just heartbreaking. Because I finally realized what my son saw when he looked at me. He saw me as a person that committed one of the worst acts that human beings can commit, which is to take another person's life. He saw me as a monster.

◆

And at that point, I realized that I had to do something different. I remember sitting there, having a conversation with myself, realizing this is not the human being I was raised to be. And I realized that if I ever got out of prison, I refused to leave as an animal, as a savage.

So I started writing a journal. I wrote when I was angry. I wrote down the things that happened with my mother, the things I experienced in the streets and growing up. It was really about getting my thoughts out so I could see them.

And then I would go back and read my thoughts. And I was like, this is the most absurd stuff you can imagine. Like, this is not how normal human beings think. I discovered so much about myself. I discovered that I had started a whole lot of stuff but never really completed anything other than a GED.

So I challenged myself to write a book.

I started to structure my days in solitary confinement like a classroom; I would study political science and philosophy in the morning, and then write for the rest of the afternoon and evening.

I ended up publishing my first novel from prison in 2008. It was called *Crack: Volume 1*. I would write everything on pads, and send them out to my family on the outside, and be like, copy this and send them to these different publishers.

I kept writing. By 2010, I had finished a few novels, worked on a project with the people who did *Chicken Soup for the Soul*, and coproduced a children's book for children with incarcerated parents. I had several job offers on the table if I was paroled. I was prepared for a life after prison. I went up in front of the parole board, but they denied me. I was devastated. I told myself I would never go in front of the parole board again, but my family convinced me otherwise.

A few months passed, and the parole board ended up calling me back early. I didn't have to wait a whole year, which is the normal process. About three weeks after I saw them again, I was walking back from the gym when an officer stopped me and told me I was getting out of prison in sixty days. I didn't want to believe him. What if he's wrong?

I was released from prison on June 22, 2010, one day after my thirty-eighth birthday. I remember walking around the track outside where we would have recreation time. While I was walking I was thinking about what this all means. At that point, I had nineteen years in. I had spent basically half of my life in prison, and I just knew I was coming out to a very different world.

✦

I moved in right away with my wife and my son. I started grinding nonstop—hitting up local bookstores, volunteering in schools, talking about writing. I wanted to reach out to these kids, make sure they didn't make the same decisions that I made that led me to prison. I created a nonprofit called Heart of the Matter, where we would go into schools and encourage kids to write about what's going on in their everyday lives. They would write about gun violence, physical and sexual abuse, drug culture—you name it. These kids were living your worst nightmares.

I was volunteering when my nephew was shot. He was driving in a car with a childhood friend when it happened. After he was shot, he got out of the car and he was just laying on the ground, bleeding to death. And people were just driving past; initially, nobody would stop to help. Eventually someone took him to the hospital. His friend died right there.

When we got to the hospital I was just standing there, standing with him, and all his friends came to visit—young

kids from the neighborhood. They were riled up, saying, "We gotta find out who did it," things like that. They were already planning revenge. And I'm looking at all these cats and I see that they've got on "Rest in Peace" T-shirts. It turns out a different young guy in their neighborhood had just been killed not too long ago.

That did it. These cats were mourning one young man, they were at the hospital bed of another young man, and they were already planning revenge on a third young man. I was like, damn, this is a fascinating statement. This is where we're at? At that point, I knew I was going to change the name of my program from Heart of the Matter to Live in Peace.

The idea was to replace all the "Rest in Peace" T-shirts in the 'hood with "Live in Peace" T-shirts. But I really wanted to impart the Live in Peace ideology to the kids. You know, when you're resting, you're laying down, you're chilling, or you're dead. You ain't getting much accomplished. But to live, you have to be very proactive. Living is more than merely existing.

What I find is that so many people in our community just exist. They're just going through day to day. But living is more than existing. You have to be very proactive. You've got to make something happen. You've got to engage people, and connect with people. You have to share spirits. That's living to me. It's what changed my life.

✦

Growing up in cities like Detroit and Chicago and Philadelphia and Baltimore is really tough. Many times the limitations that we place on ourselves are based on how we think about what we're worthy of. But once you begin to understand that your thoughts have power—like real power—that makes a difference. You realize that if you put those thoughts into the universe, you're going to attract whatever you think about most.

And if it's a bunch of negativity, failure, and excuses, that's what you will attract. If it's about positive, infinite possibilities, then you will realize how powerful a being you are and you'll start moving in that life.

I've been around people who told me everything that I wouldn't be able to accomplish as a result of being incarcerated. And I've proven them wrong every step of the way, becoming an MIT Media Lab Fellow, giving a TED Talk, teaching a class at the University of Michigan. All within three years of being released. I don't think in terms of limitation. I think in terms of infinite possibilities. BMe Community was the first organization to publicly acknowledge me as an asset to society in 2012 before any of those other titles came along.

A lot of people ask me, are you scared to go back to prison? I'm like, dude, I served half my life in prison, I can survive prison; that's not a scary world to me. For me, the motivating factor is realizing that I'm a human being who grew up in some unfortunate circumstances and made some poor decisions. I refuse to allow that to define me for the rest of my life. I just refuse to allow that to dictate what I can and cannot do.

I want to use my story as much as possible to tear down those barriers. I'm really passionate about being an example for the guys and giving them hope. 'Cause hope, man—hope is the saving grace.

Dr. Eddie Connor

AGE: 32

TITLE: Author; College Professor;
International Speaker; BMe Leader

COMMUNITY: Detroit, MI

In 1998, when I was fifteen, I started experiencing chest pains. At first I didn't talk about it with anyone, I kept it inside. As men, that's what we do: we mask the pain, we hide it behind a false sense of machismo. That's what I was doing. My mom sensed that something was wrong, but I kept denying it.

One day the pain became too hard to bear. I was watching the 1998 Rose Bowl on TV at a friend's house. By halftime, I couldn't breathe. It literally felt like somebody was stabbing me in my chest or like somebody was stomping on my heart.

I was rushed to the hospital, where they took a CT scan of my chest and discovered a blockage around my heart, my trachea, my esophagus, and my larynx. They immediately took me into surgery. I learned later that the doctors could see my cells dividing with their naked eyes.

I felt great after the surgery. I said to the doctor, "All right,

Doc. Let's get me out of here." But the doctor reported that I had an abnormal tumor. He said, "You have what we call NHL." I'm thinking to myself, "NHL? Am I going to be the youngest owner of a National Hockey League team? I don't even like the sport. What in the world is NHL?" And he told me that I had non-Hodgkins lymphoma. "You have cancer. Not stage one. Not stage two. Not stage three, but stage four cancer." I was thinking that cancer was something old people got. Not a young person like me.

I said to the doctor, "This is a death sentence." And I'll never forget his response: "Don't ask why." He meant that the focus had to be on the future, not on the past, or the why. Now, he was my physician—not my psychologist—and I was young, so that's exactly what I kept asking for the next eighteen months: "Why me, why now?"

✦

I was born in metro Detroit to two educators. Both my parents were very active in the church, and when I was six years old, we did a two-year mission in Jamaica.

That was a formative experience for me. It exposed me to the extreme poverty and deprivation that characterized the part of Kingston in which we worked. It also gave me a chance to experience a real diversity of cultures—Europeans, Asians, black people of different varieties, speaking different dialects. My brother and I studied in the British education system while there and also felt closer to my father's West Indian roots. The experience was pivotal for me.

When we returned to Detroit, I was out of step with my peers. I'd gotten a really good education for those two years, and so the administration at my school wanted to move me ahead two grades. I'd become a big fan of soccer. I'd even managed to pick up a Jamaican accent. I was ostracized from my

peer group, who were thinking, "What is this young black kid from America doing with a Jamaican accent?"

✦

Being ostracized like this was tough, but it was nothing compared to what came next. My mother and father divorced. The courts determined that I would stay with my mother and my brother would live with my father. It was painful to have the family torn apart like that. My father had visitation rights, but his visits were few and far between. I dealt with a lot of anger and bitterness and resentment because my father was not in my life. I took it all pretty rough.

My maternal grandfather, Harry Smith, lived several hours away in Jackson, Michigan. Though I didn't see him a lot, he had a powerful effect on me when we were together. He was a father-like figure for me, especially when my dad left.

Harry grew up in the South, the son of sharecroppers. He was extremely personable. He'd say hello to people in the street and I'd ask if he knew them and he'd say no. He was just like that. He never met a "stranger"; he never had a church, but wherever he went he took God with him. My grandfather was also a gentleman who imparted the importance of treating people with respect, and of respecting oneself. He was the person who taught me how to tie a tie. He taught me how to connect with people. He also had a mild-mannered wisdom. He would talk sometimes about growing up in Paris, Texas, and the discrimination and hardship he faced. He overcame those obstacles and impressed upon me that I could overcome obstacles too. I would need that sense of drive.

✦

The eighteen months after my cancer diagnosis were hell on earth. I had chemotherapy and radiation five days a week. It

was unbelievably challenging. If I thought I was ostracized upon my return from Jamaica, now I really knew what being isolated and ostracized was. People I thought were with me forsook me. My own biological father never visited me one day in the hospital. Even to this day, the thought of him not visiting makes me cringe.

My mother was stalwart in her support. She told me, "Eddie, you have to take off the pity party hat. You have to live through dying places." She always gave me a scripture: Psalm 118:17, which says, "I shall not die, but live, and declare the works of the Lord." Faith in God and the loving support of my mother really helped me to overcome that situation.

I didn't attend school for my entire sophomore year. I did the homebound study program. My homebound study teacher's name was Mrs. Whinham. She would come by our house once a week to drop off materials and go through lessons with me. She kept me on track academically. In an unlikely twist, her husband, Mr. Whinham, helped me get back on track emotionally.

Mr. Whinham took me under his wing. He was the only positive male role model that I had at that time outside of my grandfather. He was the first white man I really had any meaningful contact with, but he looked beyond my skin color, he looked beyond my race, he looked beyond the disease that I was facing. He gave me the belief that I could overcome the adversity.

While I was battling through chemo, Mr. Whinham would take me out for lunch and for walks in the neighborhood. He took me to my first baseball game, opened up a new world to me. All the while, he shared key steps and principles for how to get through. He'd say, "I'm not your father, but I am a mentor. I do care about you and I do want to see you be successful. You can beat this disease."

✦

When I got to the place where I began to change my perception and perspective about my fate, I began to see that the first three letters in cancer are "CAN," and that mind-set—to overcome, to live through dying places—propelled me forward.

I went back to school, and despite being out for a year, I graduated on time with my class. My guidance counselor looked at my cumulative GPA of 2.8 and told me, "You're not going to college, much less getting a degree. You might as well pick up a trade or go to community college." I used that as motivation to prove her and everyone else wrong. I was accepted to Eastern Michigan University and even received a $5,000 scholarship from an anonymous donor who to this day has never identified him- or herself.

I majored in education at Eastern Michigan University. While there, I worked at the Dr. King–Cesar Chavez–Rosa Parks College Days Program, where I was a mentor to at-risk youth. These were kids who didn't even have a concept of college, much less ever walk the halls of one.

I felt my calling in life materializing before me. Three days after graduation, I was substitute teaching in my former school district. I was a standout sub, particularly because of the way I could connect with young men. I was hired full-time at University High School, where I've been teaching for ten years.

While I've been teaching, I have gotten a master's degree from Marygrove College, where I am now a professor, and I have attained my PhD from the University of Michigan extension program. Studying for my master's, I really began to see the interconnection between illiteracy and incarceration. I began to understand that thirty million Americans are functionally illiterate. Sixty percent of Detroit residents are functionally illiterate. Most people in prisons can't read above a fourth-grade reading level.

I began to see that if we can flip this around, ensuring that Black and Hispanic young people develop a love of reading, we can address the issue of incarceration and all that it means in terms of the breaking apart of our communities.

✦

That brings me to Boys 2 Books, the nonprofit that I founded and run. It's a literacy program, but it is much more—it's a vehicle for mentoring young men. W. E. B. DuBois talked about the "Talented Tenth"; Boys 2 Books is investing into the other 90 percent.

The program brings young men together in a group. I underscore the importance of literacy and invite them in by introducing them to culturally relevant literature—literature in which they can see their own lives. If they like LeBron James, I'll give them a LeBron James biography. If they like hip-hop, I'll give them a book about their favorite rapper. They say, "You know what? Reading is not that bad at all." This first biography exposes them to the genre of biographies in general, and biographies take them to self-help and improvement. Self-help and improvement may take them to relevant literature around African culture, which enables them to gain an understanding of who they are. And so literacy becomes an entry point to the development of life skills, which in turn transitions them to leadership.

We also bring in guest speakers—entrepreneurs, coaches, athletes—and we do a weekly session called Circle of Brotherhood. We'll talk about male issues—hygiene, puberty, interactions with girls. We'll talk about the importance of networking, how to be a professional, how to enunciate your words. We'll talk about the difference between success and significance. It may sound funny, but one of the big things I focus on is how these young men present themselves, how they dress. Part of

this is teaching them to tie a tie. We'll laugh, joke, sometimes guys will cry. These efforts are really about broadening our young men's horizons, building their self-esteem and sense of possibility, building the life skills they need to move ahead.

Boys 2 Books fills a void that many boys have, one that I certainly felt growing up. Many of them see me as a surrogate father, a proxy for their father who is absent in their life. My grandfather and Mr. Whinham played important roles in my life, particularly during my darkest time, but I didn't have a solid, consistent mentor growing up. I definitely didn't have a father figure. The program allows me to speak back to myself when I was thirteen, fourteen, fifteen, sixteen years old.

◆

A few years after my disease, I bumped into a guy at a convenience store who I knew growing up. He didn't even say hi, he just said: "I thought you were dead." He knew what I had gone through with cancer. Standing there in the store and hearing those words made me believe that I could overcome any obstacles, even if people doubted me.

I believe this philosophy applies to our young men, as well. When I think about the future, I see the path to community-building through literacy. We've got to promote books instead of prison bars, we've got to promote jobs instead of jails. We've got to push our young men not to do four years in a prison house but four years at Morehouse. Not four years in jail but four years at Cornell and Yale.

This is my crusade: to empower our young men to read. I often quote Harry Truman, who said not all readers will be leaders, but all leaders must be readers.

Ben Jealous

AGE: 42

TITLE: Partner, Kapor Capital; former President and CEO, NAACP

COMMUNITY: Baltimore, MD

In order to lead you must be able to evaluate situations and you must be able to take risks. When you are a movement leader, or a leader in many other forms of public service, the risks can be hard to ignore. Every time you speak out on a controversial issue, you risk being publicly criticized and condemned. Every time you hold a march or demonstration, you are putting yourself and often the people you lead in risk—of arrest, violence, or worse. Some days, the police tell you that someone wants to kill you.

I was blessed to learn early in life how to weigh risk versus reward, as well as the triumph of seeking victory despite apparent dangers.

My family's doctors worried that I was going to die multiple times before I was three years old. When I was two, I was diagnosed with epilepsy. At times, I went into statis seizures,

seizing every fifteen minutes. Each grand mal seizure was powerful enough to kill me, or at least give me extensive brain damage. My doctors prescribed heavy barbiturates, which held the seizures at bay but also interrupted my ability to dream and affected my balance, so that I couldn't ride a bike.

Six years after my diagnosis, with my parents' support, I took my first major risk: I decided to stop taking the drugs. There was a possibility that the seizures could come back, and that they could return worse than before. However, not only did the seizures not come back for a decade, but I was able to learn to ride a bike and share that with my friends. It proved to be a risk work taking.

My next object lesson in calculated risk began when I was in the third grade. I grew up in Pacific Grove, California, a small coastal community in the years between its old heyday as a fishing village and its new one as a tourist destination. Neither my friends nor I came from families that had lots of money. However, that didn't bother us. We were able to entertain ourselves by playing baseball, exploring the local forest, and riding the waves at the local beach. It was a kind of haven in that way.

When I was eight, my sister's friend was eaten by a shark. To this day, he is the only surfer to have been eaten in California—not just attacked, but killed outright. It was a great white, estimated at eighteen to twenty-three feet long, and it leapt up from below the water and bit right through him. He was a kneeboarder. They said the shark probably mistook him for a seal because of the silhouette his board and fins made on the surface.

Our little surfing community always suspected there were dragons in the waves. There were sightings, and there were days we stayed out of the water because it just "felt sharky." But now we had confirmation that the dragons were real and truly deadly.

Nonetheless, one by one the older boys went back to the

waves, and in time many of us followed them. By the time I was twelve I'd got my first wet suit, fins, and board and taken to the waves. It meant learning to hold your breath for minutes underwater, and figuring out how to find the surface after your board had gone "over the falls" on a cloudy day. And ultimately it meant suiting up the same way at the same beach and casting a similar silhouette as my sister's friend. Nonetheless, I kept seeking bigger waves. By the middle of high school I had ridden waves that were almost as tall as my house. Every time I found one with a glassy face and perfect line, I knew the risk was worth it.

In high school I started taking risks on behalf of other people. When I was fourteen, I asked my father to take me to the local organizing meeting for Jesse Jackson's 1988 campaign for president. The lead organizer told the room that he was looking for someone to organize local students for a voter registration drive. My dad whispered to me that I was the only high school student in the room. I volunteered. It would mean getting over fears associated with both being the shortest person in my high school class and having a bad stutter. But after my team had registered more than a thousand new voters, I was more focused on the promise of organizing and politics than on any personal fears of rejection.

When I went to college at Columbia University, I learned that the calculus of risk is not always an either/or equation. Sometimes you both win the reward and pay the price risked in the process.

Shortly after arriving at Columbia I joined the student council. During a council meeting my sophomore year, we were informed that the school's administration had plans to end their full-need financial aid and need-blind admissions policies. Each of those policies had helped thousands of students from working families attend the school, including myself.

Moreover, the administration intended to take a vote in secret. The student council member who told us had been sworn to secrecy. She broke her vow and informed the council because she feared what the decision could mean for future generations.

Along with a number of other student council leaders, I organized a delegation of about twelve students, many also on financial aid, to walk into the Administration Building, where leaders of the faculty and administration were discussing the resolution. When we arrived, we were met with security guards, who immediately started to chain the door to the building.

At that point, we raised the ante. We fanned out, going from class to class and dorm to dorm to pull together more students to protest the pending vote. But when we returned with a delegation of more than two hundred students, we were still locked out, and we were not sure the administrators could hear us.

So we took things up another notch.

My friend Noah Potter, a kung-fu nut, scaled the iron lattice at the side of the building, looking for a way in. When he found a window, I shouted up to him and asked if it was unlocked. He pushed it up and yelled "It's open!" as he leapt inside. I scrambled up next. Others followed.

We were stuck. Security barricaded the door to the office, locking us inside. They said we would be suspended or expelled. We argued that we were fighting for families like theirs, and like our own. They pointed out the meeting was almost over and we were wasting our time.

We said we would leave if they got us a guarantee of amnesty for any protest activities that day. They got it. We took it.

So we exited the building, and locked the administration and faculty in. We wanted to give the administrators some time to think about what they were doing.

That day the protests were on CNN. The next day, we were on the front page of the *New York Times* Metro section: the

students who locked Columbia University's administration in their own building. Thanks to the attention, an alumnus named John Kluge decided to write a check to save the financial aid program. At the time, he was one of the richest men in the world. Decades earlier, he had attended our college on financial aid. He had not forgotten.

We saved the program, but we also had targets on our heads. Many administrators wanted to punish us, but between their promise and the involvement of the university's wealthiest alumnus, they were loath to do so.

The following year, they took their revenge. The university had announced that it was going to tear down a human rights landmark—the Audubon Ballroom. Many in the community considered its floors sacred. After all, it was the place where Marcus Garvey had held some of his largest meetings. It was where Malcolm X was assassinated. The stains from his blood were said to still be on the floor.

Many of the same group of student leaders organized a protest. This time the university's president seized the opportunity to target the "ringleaders" of the financial aid protests. He set up a kangaroo court, appointing one alumnus as our sole judge and juror. He ultimately gave four of us, myself included, a one-semester suspension. We were the first four students suspended from Columbia University for political protests in almost two decades.

I left Harlem and made a pilgrimage to Mississippi, where there was organizing work to be done. The governor at the time was trying to close down two out of three historically black public colleges and turn one of them into a prison. The third was to be made majority-white within two years. There was to be no increase in spaces for black students at the state's historically white schools.

Just like at Columbia, I was outraged at the possibility of

hundreds or even thousands of students of color and low-income students losing access to higher education. I was told my job was to organize "New York City–style street protests" to draw attention to the cause and make public opposition more visible.

The death threats started pretty quickly. I had arrived in Mississippi to help organize the biggest civil rights protests the state had seen in a very long time just as Byron De La Beckwith was going on trial. The notorious criminal was facing murder charges—three decades too late—for the assassination of Medgar Evers.

At one point, one of his fellow white supremacists put word out publicly that if De La Beckwith was convicted and sent to prison, one of our lead organizers would be killed in retribution. I was one of the lead organizers. This was something I had not dealt with before. At Columbia I was putting my education at risk, but in Mississippi I was dealing with a risk to my life.

My colleagues and I remained steadfast despite the threats. The community came out to support our marches and protests in increasing numbers. We won. The schools are open to this day.

I ultimately stayed in Mississippi for much longer. I hung up my marching boots for a while and became an investigative reporter at the *Jackson Advocate* newspaper. It was the most frequently firebombed publication in the country. My beat was public corruption. The last reporter who had it said he had paid a dear price.

I would go on to write stories that were credited with helping to free the wrongfully convicted and save the lives of whistle-blowers who had been targeted for their courage. The new job came with new risks and new enemies. Still, it was easy to stay.

I was a long way from my university, but still I was in the midst of the best teachers I have ever known:

From Chokwe Lumumba, the attorney and future mayor of Jackson who always defended the poorest defendants with the most daunting obstacles to proving their innocence, I learned how to stand up for the wrongfully accused.

From James Anderson, who had built much of the state's public health system and one of its most powerful political machines, I learned how to build powerful grassroots political organizations.

From Dr. Aaron Henry, who spent decades defining the mission of the Mississippi NAACP as its leader, I learned that you should not fear the people who tell you they are going to kill you.

From Henry Kirksey, who made fair representation for all Mississippians through equitable redistricting his life goal, I learned that we could control the system rather than having the system control us.

From Alvin Chambliss, who argued some of the most important civil rights cases in Mississippi's history, I learned that before you can prevail in the court of law, you must prevail in the court of public opinion.

Of all my mentors, the one who had perhaps the greatest impact was Charles Tisdale. Mr. Tisdale was the publisher of the *Jackson Advocate*, and he had dealt with the threats and the firebombs. Mr. Tisdale taught me to write by handing me back news story drafts that were bleeding with red ink and corrections. He also taught me how to manage the deadly virus that is mortal fear.

When I was still in my early twenties I was writing one of the most important stories of my life, about a man who was facing his third trial for arson. I was able to get confessions from the sheriff and a lawyer who were involved in framing him. I started getting threats from people close to the sheriff, and the threats were getting specific.

I went to Mr. Tisdale and laid my fears at his feet. He looked at me and said, "Son, I just have one question for you. Do you feel like you're doing what God's calling you to do?" When I said I did, he asked, "Then who are you more afraid of? Them fools, or God himself?"

After he put it in those terms, I got right back to work.

All of the men who mentored me took on tremendous risks. They knew they were eligible for attack by the Klan or other lesser-known terrorists who were still very active in the South. And like we learned as children at that beach in California, they also knew their fears were well substantiated. Indeed, even more so—they all knew men who had been killed or assassinated, some of whom had been their closest friends. Their lives had forced them to both calculate the odds and consider the possible rewards. They had long since decided that there were no higher rewards than freedom, equality, and dignity, and that the risks were worth it.

For me, that was the greatest lesson I learned from them: if you choose to live life beyond your fears, you will never have to live wondering what could have been.

✦

As president of the NAACP, part of my job was inspiring others to take great risks. However, oftentimes it was the people I was supposedly leading who inspired me.

I remember one day in 2011 I was at the head of a March against Fear in Spokane, Washington. It was just months after a man had been arrested for planting a bomb at the local NAACP's MLK Day parade along that same route.

When I wanted to take a short walk, the police asked that I stay put instead. They explained they would have to reposition a dozen antiterrorism snipers if I did so. I agreed.

However, when they asked me to wear body armor because

they said I was at special risk, I asked if the kids in the march were being issued body armor too. They said no.

I refused to wear the armor.

Those kids had decided that the reward of living a life beyond fear was worth risking any bad thing that could happen that day.

I wanted to be like them.

Reverend Tony Lee

AGE: 46

TITLE: Founder and Pastor, Community of Hope A.M.E. Church

COMMUNITY: Prince George's County, MD

When people ask me what I preach in my sermons, my answer is always the same: hope. Hope is the evidence of God's existence. With hope comes the possibility of transformation. When you take away a person's hope, you sabotage their faith. So, I preach hope.

I'm the pastor at Community of Hope Church. We're located in Prince George's County—known as one of the most affluent black communities in the country. But, let me be clear, we're located *inside* the Beltway, where all of the social indicators are at red—high murder rate, high poverty, rampant drug use. Our community is the unchurched, the uncommitted. We tell our congregants to come as you are—doesn't matter what you did last night or even this morning, come as you are. We believe in hope and in transformation, and my own story relates to this as well.

✦

I didn't come from a broken home like many brothers in DC. I grew up in a close-knit household in Prince George's County. My mother and father had a very loving relationship and shared responsibilities according to their strengths.

I dreaded the start of each school year. With the fall, I knew conflict would come into our household. I was in the gifted and talented program in school, but I was a horrible student. I was bored and always mouthing off to teachers, so they couldn't stand me. I can remember many a year when I had to have a behavior form completed by teachers each day to show my parents how I'd handled myself.

By the second marking period, my parents would see my report card with all Cs and that would be it. When I was young, I'd get beatings. When I was older, I'd lose privileges and be placed on restriction. But even in their discipline, they kept affirming me. They would say, "We wouldn't be mad at you if you brought in a D or an F, and you had a D or F mind. But you have an A mind." And so there was something in me that knew that no matter how low I fell, I had in me what it took to get back up.

When I say I got into trouble, it was never major dirt. It wasn't like I was a Crip or something like that. But I had serious anger issues. You kind of had to be angry to survive DC in the late eighties and early nineties, when the crack epidemic hit and the city became the murder capital of the country. I also liked to party in the DC go-go scene. I drank a lot and got into fights. I even got locked up once for stealing.

My approach to college was pretty similar to my approach to high school. I was accepted to University of Maryland on the strength of my high SAT scores, not my high school grades. Once at College Park, I figured out just what I needed to do to

get by and did just that. I was told I would be put on academic probation if I had a 1.78 GPA, so I maintained a 1.79.

After my freshman year I switched my major to agribusiness, and I got exposure to some of the pan-Africanist thinkers. I guess you could say that I started developing a sense of consciousness at this time. I started growing, developing. This is when I began to go for something more for myself.

Transformation is not instantaneous. It is not linear. It's something that zigs and zags, moves forward and backward. I might want to say that I was beginning to move in the right direction, but as I came to my senior year in college, I had one especially transformative moment that would reflect just how low one can sink.

My brother is the closest person to me in the world, the person I love the most. He's four years younger than me, and we've worked together as colaborers each step of the way. When I'm down, he has always said, "Come on, let's put our shoulder to the plow together."

During my senior year we got into a small dispute—I can't even remember what it was over—and I actually tried to kill him. I tried to choke him to death. At the last minute I came to my senses and dropped my hands. That was when I realized I really had an anger problem. My fuse had gotten so short that I could come close to killing the person with whom I am the closest, the person I love the most. This was my lowest point. But it was also a turning point.

Ironically, it was around this time that my brother gave me the greatest gift he's given me. When he was a senior in high school, he found an Ebenezer A.M.E. Church near his school. We'd grown up going to church, but in my teenage and young adult years, I'd slipped away. My brother persuaded me to check out the new church he'd found and I did. We started attending the church together.

There was something about the way this pastor spoke that really connected with me. This pastor, Rev. Dr. Grainger Browning, was talking about a relationship with Christ, not just the rules. He was also talking about a liberation theology. He was talking about how God changes us so we can help change our neighborhoods and our communities and our society. I hadn't heard the gospel shared like that before and it moved me.

One Sunday, I was sitting in the pew listening to Pastor Browning deliver a sermon. He said, "Some of you are being called to the ministry." In my mind I said, "Well I don't feel a call to ministry, but I feel a call to be a leader in the black community." And as soon as I thought that, he said, "Others of you just told yourself that you feel like God is calling you to be a leader in the black community." It was exactly what I was thinking. Mind you, I was still drinking heavily and partying, but at that moment, I felt that I could be a leader in the community.

I always say that "the calling" is an unfolding, a process, just like personal transformation. After I graduated from college, I worked at the Small Business Administration. I even started my own business. I thought I was going to build a career managing rappers. Then I started volunteering in the youth ministry at Ebenezer, and something just went off inside of me.

I knew this was where I was supposed to be. Within a month I quit my job and started working at a place called Sasha Bruce Youthwork. I worked directly with some of the most at-risk youth in DC—homeless kids, kids in the sex trade, those deep into drugs. I was a substance abuse prevention coordinator, which meant I went into schools and neighborhoods all over DC to tell young people about the challenges of drugs. I'd been in almost every hood in DC while I was growing up. The kids in schools could relate to me.

◆

That was the easier side of the job. I would also be out on drug strips talking to young people about drugs, right where dudes were selling drugs. It was the craziest thing in the world.

I recognized that I had unique gifts to build our ministry to meet the needs of Generations X and Y. After working with my brother to build the youth ministry at Ebenezer to three thousand people at a ten-thousand-person church, I felt called to pastor. The presiding elder at the A.M.E. Church recognized my unique gifts and skill set, and he asked me to start a church: Community of Hope.

We felt led to place Community of Hope inside the Beltway in Prince George's County because we wanted to be where the need was greatest. We saw people being pushed out of DC due to gentrification, and they were landing inside the Beltway in Prince George's.

We started with eight charter members on Easter Sunday in 2006. Our first location was in a nightclub that had stripper nights. The club would close at 4 A.M. and we would start at ten. We focused on the unchurched, the uncommitted. As we envisioned it, our target demographic groups were those who had never been to church or who hadn't been to church in years.

We are a dress-as-you-are church. We have a line we say every Sunday morning: "We don't care who you are, what you've done, or who you did it with. We don't care if you did it last night or woke up doing it this morning, but when you get here you're in the right place at the right time to become all that God has called you to be."

✦

We are a holistic ministry, and our outreach areas are focused: violence prevention, education, and HIV/AIDS. On violence prevention, we focus on brokering truces between crews in rival neighborhoods. We do work with the police department and

different community organizations, and we are able to focus on young people who are facing challenges. Now when the police are having some issues in our area—if there's a shooting—we get the call. We've been able to help ease tensions.

In terms of our other focus areas, we try to reach people where they are. For example, we have an HIV and AIDS Ministry. We do club tours in which we'll go to the clubs and either hand out harm reduction materials or even do testing at the club.

I believe we have had a transformative impact on the lives of many of our congregants. We've had cats who've come out of jail and gotten jobs, adopted more productive lifestyles. We've had parents who started attending our church when their kids were just out of lockup. The kids now are in college and on the path to productive lives.

Community of Hope outgrew the nightclub in about nine months, and now we're located in the Iverson Mall. We have a little over three thousand members.

✦

There's important work ahead. We need to reclaim the narrative around black men. We need to move from all of the negatives and dysfunction that make up the dominant public narrative, and start highlighting the fact that there are black men who are attempting to succeed. Black men who are working, raising their children, who are fathers, who are husbands, who are community contributors, who are really moving our community forward in a way that should be applauded.

It all comes back to hope. The scripture talks about the fact that faith is the substance of things hoped for, the evidence of things not seen. Hope is essential. If people lose hope, it can sabotage their faith. Whatever I do, I try to help hurting people find hope.

Emmanuel Cephas

AGE: 32

TITLE: Computer Scientist; Physicist;
Inventor; Founder, Human Storm, LLC;
BMe Leader

COMMUNITY: Baltimore, MD

I have always had an almost maniacal drive to understand the world, understand the universe, and understand the future.

I grew up in Baltimore, Maryland, under difficult circumstances. My mom and dad separated when I was young. My mother suffered from schizophrenia and wasn't able to take care of us. She died when I was in college, and I'd only seen her a few times over the years after we moved in with my father. My siblings and I went to live with my dad full-time when I was in fifth grade.

My dad worked as a welder. He'd work overtime as though it were nothing. I've never seen someone with a more intense work ethic than my father. He also always put a strong emphasis on education. He would pay us $5 for every A we got on our report cards.

Though he cared for us deeply, my dad struggled with drug addiction, and this heightened dangerous contradictions in

him. He wanted me to do great in school, but he would also call me a "dumb fuck" if I didn't do something small, like make his lunch correctly or clean up perfectly. My dad was proud of me, but he envied me. He would search for the slightest opportunity to remind me that even though I was book smart, I was really dumb and had no common sense. Even though my dad would never let anyone hurt us, eventually he hurt us.

✦

The summer before my freshmen year of college, I pulled a stunt to rescue my brother, sister, and me from my dad. I was able to get us emancipated by filing a detailed report of our circumstances at home and getting a protective order against my father. During summer of the year 2000, I was able to get my siblings and myself out of my father's clutches before I would have had to take our safety into my own hands. One statement I put in the letter to the judge was "If we do not receive help, then I will have to make the choice . . . him, or us." I did that because I assumed if I took matters into my own hands, then I would get caught, so I wanted a paper trail back to the judge so that they would know that I had tried to do this by lawful means.

Until high school, my aunt was the mother figure in my life. She was my father's sister, and she took us in in 1996 when I was thirteen and my dad was in jail. Living with her in a two-bedroom town house with a family of eight, lots of roaches, and little money—times were tough. But she did her best to care for me and my siblings. Although she was struggling with a drug addiction herself, she was there for us as much as possible. She didn't have a car, so she used to walk miles with me to my high school just to watch me run at a cross-country meet. I love my aunt like a mother. I dedicate Tupac's lyric to her, "And even as a crack fiend, mama/You always was a black queen, mama."

I found my escape in my imagination and my ability to really throw myself into a subject. Science fiction was my first real love. In many ways it was a precursor to the work I do now in science and technology.

✦

My dad introduced me to science fiction. I developed my early obsession by sitting at my dad's side watching science fiction movies. To this day, those are some of my fondest childhood memories.

I was very good at drawing, and so I would conjure worlds of robots, transformers, and UFOs, and draw them for hours on end. If you saw my room, you would see that every space on the wall was covered with drawings and paintings of science fiction imagery. I remember being fascinated by the cyborg in *The Terminator*—half-robot, half-skeleton, fascinated by the fact that he'd come back from the future, that he was an integration of technology and human form.

In middle school, unbeknownst to anyone, I'd go to the library on my own and check out every science fiction book I could find. This was during the time when my dad was in prison. Back at home I would scrutinize each page, hoping to find the one line that explained how I could control objects with my mind, how I could levitate a pencil in school. I got into concepts of extraterrestrials, alien abduction, telekinetics, and time travel.

✦

In the early years of high school, I was known mainly as a good student and a great artist and dancer. As far as academics, I was in the gifted and talented program starting in sixth grade. I had a dance crew that was making a little noise in Baltimore. My home life was still chaotic and in flux, and given the challenges

my siblings and I faced, I felt like my output at school during the early years of high school was pretty impressive.

Then in junior year, in astronomy class, I had an epiphany. I developed an overnight explosive passion and determination to be a scientist. It felt like it came out of nowhere.

My teacher that year was Tyler Bradley. The first day I showed up in his class, there were all these cool pictures on the wall with cool names like "Eagle Nebula." I'd ask him, "What is this? Did someone draw this or do it through graphic design?" He informed me that they were images taken by satellite, from the Hubble Telescope, and that they showed different bodies in the universe. Now, as a kid, I'd learned about the planets and the sun, but that was it. With the images that Hubble was transmitting back, there was so much more to see. We were learning that there were thousands of millions of galaxies, billions of stars, that the size of the earth compared to the sun was the same as a marble compared to Baltimore. As I learned how vast the universe is, my mind ignited like the big bang.

I was on the edge of my seat. I mean, it was amazing. So I asked Mr. Bradley, "Have we traveled to any of those stars? Any of those planets?" And he said, "No, they're too far away." I asked, "Why don't we do what they did in *Star Trek*—travel at warp speed?" He started laughing. "That's not real. It's impossible."

I just couldn't believe it. I thought that technology was technology. There was no limit; it was just a matter of waiting for someone to build it. Mr. Bradley explained the laws of physics and the impossibility of traveling faster than the speed of light. I asked, "Who is this Physics and why does he set the laws?" He explained that physics is the area of science that deals with space, time, and motion, and he showed me math equations that describe the world and the universe, that tell you what you can and can't do.

I was bowled over by the idea that you could explain aspects of the universe with math, but I was also amazed at the fact that there was so much that was still unknown. It all brought me back to my early fascination with science fiction and the questions I grappled with as a younger kid.

Within two weeks, I had a complete plan. I was going to solve the riddle of how to achieve interstellar space travel.

✦

I interned at NASA three times while I completed a bachelor's in physics at the University of Maryland, and in computer science at Frostburg State University. I worked at NASA for two years before pursuing a PhD program in computer science at Virginia Tech. All of these experiences were formative for me, and they helped pave the path to where I am now.

Human Storm, LLC, is my technology start-up company. While it's not focused on solving interstellar space travel, it might just be the key to unlock the minds necessary to create that elusive technology.

My team is creating software technology that allows people to learn how to solve algebra equations without a keyboard, without a mouse, without a pen and a paper. Their body movements will cause symbols in the equation to move on the computer screen; they'll be able to manipulate the equation without touching it. The software offers a way of bringing together our natural proclivity for music and movement with a method for learning linear algebra and solving equations. It all goes back to my childhood infatuation with telekinetics, but now I have the background to wire technology together to create that kind of experience.

I invented the software with one purpose in mind: to rebrand mathematics. Before I spoke with Mr. Bradley that day in eleventh grade, when I thought about math I thought of

counting change at the store. Culturally, it has become accept-
able to say, "I can't do math" or "I'm not into math." But math
is so fundamental to everything that is happening in our society
with the evolution of technology.

✦

Look how much amazing technology is being developed by so
few people. Only 5 percent of American workers are employed
in science and engineering fields, but they're responsible for
more than 50 percent of economic expansion, as well as so
much of the amazing technology we have today. Now imagine
if 50 percent or 60 percent of our population was proficient
in math. Imagine what amazing new technologies could be
developed. That's the vision of Human Storm—to unlock our
full potential.

This is especially true when it comes to black Americans.
When I think about what has to happen for black males to be
understood as assets to our society, I think that learning math is
one key component. At a very young age, we need to have our
black males understand that they have the power to redesign
and reinvent the world.

I love what Amos Wilson said: the black man must bring
into existence a new world order. It's a bit like interstellar space
travel. We need to take those huge goals and at a very young
age start to ensure our black males understand they can achieve
them.

Barrington Irving

AGE: 30

TITLE: Pilot; Educator; Entrepreneur; Founder, Experience Aviation

COMMUNITY: Miami, FL

I was a kid who thought I wasn't good at math and science. Then at seventeen, I met a black pilot who challenged me to fly. At nineteen, I became the youngest person and the first African-American to fly solo around the world. Today, I run programs and build curricula that challenge kids to learn math and science through aviation. I try to inspire others with my story.

I was born in Kingston, Jamaica. My family moved to South Florida when I was young. We lived just a few miles from the airport, so there were always planes flying overhead.

I was lucky to live in a two-parent home, though I didn't see my parents a whole lot. They were both always working several jobs each, pushing to make sure we stayed afloat. They owned a tiny Bible bookstore, where I would sometimes work. But despite their best efforts, we were poor, and I was picked on because of it. I didn't have my first pair of Nikes until I was

in high school, 1998. I remember saving my lunch money over several months so I could afford them.

I was a muscular kid, and in high school I discovered a talent for football. I worked very hard to succeed at it. My high school was ranked number three in the nation. I began to see football as my ticket out of my neighborhood—I didn't necessarily expect to play in the NFL, but I believed I could get a scholarship and figure it out from there. Our team motto was "Failure is not an option," and I really took that to heart.

Then one day in 2001 my life changed. I was working in my family's bookstore and this black man walks in, dressed in a pilot's uniform, looking sharp as ever. I had never seen a black pilot before. He could tell I was impressed, but at first he didn't speak. Then out of the blue he said to me, "Hey son, have you ever thought about becoming a pilot?"

I looked at him like he was crazy. I told him I didn't think I was smart enough to fly a plane. He said, "If I can do it, you can do it." He introduced himself: Gary Robinson. I asked Gary, "If I became a pilot, how much money would I make?" After he answered that question, I took an interest in aviation.

✦

At the end of my senior year of high school, I received a scholarship offer to play football at the University of Florida, but I turned it down to pursue aviation. It seemed like a crazy decision to everyone, especially since my parents certainly couldn't afford to pay for college.

Aviation became my passion. I dug into books about flying planes and began to learn all that I could about it. I worked odd jobs—bagging groceries, cleaning pools—to earn the money I needed to learn to fly. I earned my first license when I was nineteen; it cost me $6,000. Once I had my license, I did local flights all around Miami, up to northern Florida. It was

amazing to get to see these other places and meet new people, experience different cultures, even if it was just around Florida.

I remember one night sitting on my bedroom floor, and a thought came to me: "What if I just flew around the world? What if I could inspire other people like me to fly, by proving that it could be done?" I looked into it, and found out that if I flew around the world solo I would be setting a record as the youngest person and first African-American to do so. It got my competitive juices flowing.

The first thing you need to fly around the world is a plane. No one wanted to rent me one, lease me one, or let me borrow one. I knew I would have to secure sponsorships, so I hit the road for two years. I received more rejections than I can count. Eventually it dawned on me that it would be cheaper to get parts donated to reduce the cost of an aircraft.

Just like with cars, there are equipment manufacturers around the country that build the various components of a plane. I figured out that the engine manufacturer I needed to reach was based in Mobile, Alabama. One Friday evening I rented a car and drove from Miami to Mobile. I slept in the car, and on Monday morning I showed up in front of one of the largest engine manufacturers for small planes in the country, Continental Motors. I said, "Hi. My name is Barrington Irving. I'd like to see if your engine's good enough for my airplane."

I met with the CEO, and at first he turned me away with a curt "Thank you for coming." Then a few weeks later, I got a call from the CEO. He told me he had studied what I was trying to do, and that if I'd had the guts to find him, he believed I would succeed. Right then and there, he sponsored an engine worth $83,000. That set everything in motion. With an engine I was able to get the cockpit system sponsored, then the seats and air-conditioning system. Ultimately I got enough parts that an airplane manufacturer, Columbia Aircraft, felt forced

to build the plane. I cut the final cost down from $650,000 to $350,000. My team and I outsmarted the industry.

<div align="center">✦</div>

Five thousand people showed up on the day of my departure. CNN interviewed me; people were carrying signs that said "Go, Barrington, Go." It was a heady moment. Meanwhile, I had no survival suit for a water landing, my plane had no weather radar, and I had a total of $30 in my pocket. I was laughing to myself thinking, "Where *am* I going?" From the outset of the project, I figured that once I applied myself and got my story out there, people along the way would believe me and support my mission. That's exactly what happened.

People will say to me, "What made you think to do that, to get your own plane built?" I tell them that when I played football, failure was never an option. It was something that was drilled into me every single day, and it stuck. There are multiple ways of accomplishing something. The hardest part is just sticking to it, being resourceful, thinking outside of the box.

<div align="center">✦</div>

The hardest thing to teach kids is to learn to fail. I became confident in my abilities, particularly my academic abilities, through the experience of learning to fly and working with planes. It was cool to see that I was good at math and science—you need to be in order to fly—despite having always assumed I wasn't smart enough, didn't have the aptitude for those subjects. I started my nonprofit, Experience Aviation, because I realized that other kids, kids we'd written off, kids who lived near the airport in Miami but had never seen a plane up close, could build their confidence in the same way.

I've started to realize that education is the only industry that doesn't know how to communicate with kids. Everyone else can

do it—Nike, Verizon, and the Gap. Everyone can communicate with our kids except the schools that are supposed to teach them.

Our philosophy is, we sell the finish line first to kids and then we educate them via math and science. Our programs engage kids in exposure to flight, but the core is around building cars and airplanes from scratch. I still remember when I said to the board, "Let's do an experiment. Let's approach sixty kids from failing schools in Miami. And let's challenge them to build an airplane from scratch in ten weeks." There was some skepticism, but the board was supportive. It was a challenge.

We've had some amazing success. For example, a group of high school students at Miami Norland and Carol City Senior High built an entire airplane from component parts in ten weeks. We also challenged middle school students to build a super car faster than a Ferrari F430 Spider. They ran into more difficulty with the car because they made some mistakes on the electrical system that set them back a few months. But they completed that too—well ahead of the twelve months that the distributor of the kit predicted it would take them.

And all the while, I could see kids problem-solving, building their confidence, building their collaborative skills—building hope. It is such a powerful thing because these kids are not learning math and science in their schools. And yet here they are applying both of those skills on a day-to-day basis, actually constructing vehicles that work. I'll never forget when they finished the plane and I was able to fly the kids around Miami. It was just Miami, the area they grew up in, but it opened new worlds to them. I was shocked because many of them had never seen the ocean before.

Failing is built into our curriculum, built into our approach. When the kids building the car ran into difficulties, we coached them but didn't tell them the answer. When it took them longer

to complete the project than first planned, they had the opportunity to do a postmortem, to determine what had worked and what hadn't worked. It was about learning from failure. And I'll say this: the six months it took them to complete the car was still a record time.

The hardest part of learning to fly a plane is learning to fail. I had to learn that when it comes to landing, it's not always going to be perfectly smooth. There's just too much going on. But when you've landed the plane, you've landed the plane, even if it's not completely smooth. And you can and you should see what worked and what didn't, so you can incorporate those lessons the next time you try to land.

Early on when I started my nonprofit I was faced with the very real question "How do I mentor kids when I'm still a kid?" But the answers became clearer as I thought about Gary Robinson and the others who took the time to mentor me. Throughout the whole process of funding and building my plane, Gary never said, "You can't do this." He said, "You can do this." And that meant the world to me.

Ron Davenport

AGE: 78

TITLE: Chairman, Sheridan
Broadcasting Corporation

COMMUNITY: Pittsburgh, PA

I grew up in North Philadelphia, Pennsylvania. My parents were working-class folks. My mother worked for the government. My stepfather worked as a cabdriver, and later in a factory. My real father died when I was two. My mother suffered from tuberculosis, so I lived with my grandmother for three years while my mother was in the sanitarium.

My family was one of the first families in the public housing project from Richard Allen Homes. The public housing program—what would be known as "the projects"—was new at the time. The Richard Allen Homes weren't segregated—they were mostly black, but there were some white families there.

As a student, I was frankly up and down. I was a good student when I chose to be and not so good when I didn't choose to be, like most kids. But when I got to high school, I decided that I had to be a better student, and then I became a very good

student. I played for the high school football team, and I was vice president of my high school and treasurer of my graduating class. I was in the top fifth as far as grades in the school. I was determined to go to college—in the social group that I ran with, everyone went to college.

I graduated from West Philadelphia High School in January 1954 and enrolled in the College of Business Administration at Penn State. At that time at Penn State, we had 11,000 students, and 120 or 125 were black. So, 1.1 percent. I remember seeing white folks sweeping the streets and telling my roommate, Matt Robinson—who is Holly Robinson Peete's father—"We are a long way from home."

✦

I was a very successful student at Penn State. I was what was then called a BMOC—a big man on campus. I belonged to several honorary student government societies, and I was president of the Youth University.

Penn State was whatever you would make of it. There was no feeling that you didn't belong. If you were there and you were taking the same courses as everybody else, then you were like everybody else. If you put yourself forward, people would judge you on the basis of what you put on the table regardless of race.

But the social life was different. At that time there were very fancy white fraternities, and on Saturday nights they'd dress up and they'd have their parties after the basketball games, and they'd go to the fraternity houses. We did not have that at first. But ultimately we rented a small house for my fraternity, Omega Psi Phi. It wasn't a prestigious address, but we had great times there. When our Saturday night came, we could go out too.

✦

My generation of African-Americans believed that we could compete with anybody. I was always taught never to use race as an excuse. If you didn't get a job, you would say that maybe it was because you were not prepared, or you didn't comb your hair right. The only excuse you would not use was that you were a Negro.

Leading up to the summer of my junior year I took eleven job interviews at different corporations. Because that's how that goes. You work for a large corporation and work your way up to the top. I did not get any follow-up. So, finally I started asking, "Do you hire Negroes for your business management trainee programs?" And they'd say, "No."

Once it became clear that I could not follow the path that I thought I was going to follow, I decided that I had to be independent and be able to take care of myself. I decided to go to law school. So I went to Temple Law School and then got a graduate law fellowship at Yale. After graduation, I had job offers from the Justice Department and the State Department. I even had a teaching offer at the University of Nigeria. In the end, I took a job as a law professor at Duquesne University. When I joined the law faculty in 1963, I was the third black hired to a white law faculty in the history of this country.

✦

In 1964, during my first year of teaching, a colleague told me about a position working on the NAACP Legal Defense Fund in New York City. I joined the LDF in the summer of 1964 and I was a part of the Mississippi Freedom Summer project. I headed the LDF office in Jackson, Mississippi, for two weeks, right when the young civil rights workers James Earl Chaney, Andrew Goodman, and Michael Schwerner went missing. During that summer I also worked on the legal brief for *Abernathy v. the State of Alabama*, which was the Freedom Riders case.

In the summer of 1966, I went to Washington, DC, to work on school desegregation for the Department of Education Civil Rights Division. I spent the entire summer of 1966 heading up a school desegregation team. I walked every hill and molehill in Mississippi meeting with the school principals and board chairs, about how we were going to go about school desegregation.

We had the power of the federal government behind us, and we could tell them what kinds of programs they were going to have. There were various plans available. One was called the Grade of the Year Plan. This was where you would desegregate one grade, then a second grade, a third and so forth and so on. Then there was a Four, Four, and Four Plan, where you would desegregate the first four years in a school, the next four years, and the last four years. And what we discovered was that every time a grade was desegregated all hell would break loose, and you know there'd be riots. So finally I came to the conclusion that what we would do would be to desegregate all twelve grades at once, and have one riot.

It was a challenging time, to say the least. One time in 1966, a school board chairman said to me, "Damn, boy, it's a good thing you weren't here last year, because you'd have been killed." I said, "Well, I'm glad I wasn't here."

✦

In 1970 I became dean of the Law School at Duquesne. When I became dean I was the first black dean of a white American Law School in the history of this country. I was thirty-four years of age, black, and a Protestant at a conservative white Catholic school.

After working in politics for four or five years, I figured that we—that is, black folks—had to own a piece of the economy. I would talk to people about doing that, and they'd look at me

like I was crazy because I was a law professor; what did I know about business?

I had friends in the business community—white corporate leaders who were smart and independent—and they were not going to let me buy a steel mill. But I knew they would lend me money to buy a business that serviced black people. So me and a group of four other blacks bought a radio station. We named it after the street on which my wife and I lived, Sheridan Avenue.

After we founded the Sheridan Broadcasting Corporation, we bought four other stations—an AM and FM in Pittsburgh, an AM in Buffalo, and then an AM in Boston. Then in 1976 we bought a half interest in the Mutual Black Network, and in 1979, we bought the other 51 percent, and changed the name from the Mutual Black Network to the Sheridan Broadcasting Network.

When I first got in the business, black radio music was called R&B, or rhythm and blues. Then when whites discovered it, it became "urban music." And all of a sudden, you'd be competing against ABC and CBS, and then other major broadcasters.

One of my first goals when I bought the station was to have announcers who spoke good English. I did not want announcers who patronized black people. White announcers would patronize blacks by talking down to them, you know, the lowest common denominator. We had newsmen who worked at making certain that the issues of black people were brought to the fore.

The white stations would never make the same commitments that we would make. They would never bring the same people on. For example, the white stations would never bring a Louis Farrakhan on. Our station would. You can't beat me where I live. It's the difference between the reality and imitation.

✦

Broadcasting is very challenging. By the nineties there were two networks that were targeted toward African-Americans. There was my Sheridan Broadcasting Network and the other was the National Black Network. After the first Gulf War hit, advertising went into the tank. It became clear to me that Sheridan could not win a two-front war—against ABC and CBS on one side, and National Black Network on the other. So after some very challenging and difficult negotiations, we combined the two companies to create the American Urban Radio Networks, which still exists.

In the early nineties my son joined the company. And then in 2001 my daughter, who has an MBA from Stanford and is a graduate of Harvard College, joined the company. Now my daughter is president of our Gospel Network. My son is president of the Radio Division, and he just received a patent for an idea that he has in terms of the Internet, and we're hopeful that it's going to be very exciting for the future of radio.

✦

I learned early on that the key to advancement is to be in the room where the decisions are made. I've focused all my life on being in that room—as a peer, not as a supplicant.

Sheridan Broadcasting allows me and the people I represent to have a voice in that room; it establishes a standard of peer relations. One story illustrates this idea. When Bill Clinton was elected to the presidency, the head of our news operations went to the White House to meet with the administration. He was greeted by an African-American man whose task was to "reach out" to the African-American community.

The first thing our head of news operations did was hand over a list of Sheridan Broadcasting affiliates, which included our estimated reach of over twenty million listeners a week. After that, it was a whole different conversation. He was intro-

duced to the inner circle of the White House, and there was hope for a relationship between my company and the administration.

✦

If you have an independent base and independent power, then people will treat you accordingly. That doesn't mean they will always do what you want. But you will get to present your ideas in a serious fashion to the people who make the decisions—not the people who advise the people who make the decisions.

Jarvis Sulcer

AGE: 45

TITLE: President and Chief Education Officer, Level Playing Field Institute

COMMUNITY: Oakland, CA

Neither one of my parents went to college. My mom was a homemaker for a large part of her life, and my dad was a Vietnam vet who worked at Exxon as a machinist for thirty-plus years. My parents raised me in a working-class neighborhood in Baton Rouge, Louisiana. They stressed faith in God and education above all. My father would always say, "Boy, you better get something in your head."

I remember the first time I discovered that I was pretty good at math. I was in Ms. Crawford's class, at an all-black elementary school in Baton Rouge. We had a competition, and I was the first person in her fourth-grade class to learn the multiplication table. I got a chocolate candy as a reward for doing well.

In middle school I did well on a math test to get into an advanced computer math class. The teachers were shocked. At first I couldn't get in the class. I would've upset the black-kids-

to-white-kids ratio. At the time, there needed to be a particular number of black kids and white kids. Thankfully, the teacher knew my father, and they ultimately let me take the course. That was the first time that I saw something impacting me academically because of the color of my skin.

When I was fourteen, I had a bit of an academic setback. I ended the first semester of my sophomore year of high school with a 1.8 cumulative GPA. Then one day, I came across this article. My mom and dad subscribed to *Ebony* and *Jet*, and there was this March 1984 issue of *Ebony* that profiled young black achievers. These young people were doing all types of things. One girl was working on a PhD in applied mathematics at Harvard, and an MS in applied mathematics from UC Berkeley. Another young lady was getting a PhD in electrical engineering at MIT.

I cut the articles out and pasted them on the wall in my dad's study. It was perfect timing. See, I didn't know any black engineers or scientists. I didn't even know any black professionals really, besides teachers. But to read about these young people who were achieving big things, I said, "Wow—that could be me." I kept that *Ebony* magazine for years, even through college. Whenever I was discouraged or did not feel like studying, I would read the story of Iris Mack, Carlton Blunt, Carol Espy, and others.

I ended up getting a full ride to study physics at Southern University. At college I began to meet more blacks, male and female, who were working on or had received PhDs. It was pretty inspirational. These were people who were not only at a lab doing innovative work, but also leading the team. They were the ones calling the shots at their companies. I noticed that a lot of these men and women got their PhDs from schools like MIT, Stanford, and Cornell. So I went to Cornell to get mine.

✦

Cornell was totally unlike Southern University. Southern is a primarily black college, and all my classes were with other black students. It was a very close-knit community. We studied together and had fun together. At Cornell, I was suddenly the only black student in a majority of my classes.

I distinctly remember one time when we were assigned a problem set, and we were supposed to work together in teams. I asked if I could join a team, and they told me to meet at a certain time and place. But they ended up changing the time and the place. I sat there for ten, fifteen, thirty minutes—in those days we didn't have cell phones. I eventually got up and went back home. They didn't want me to be in their group.

There were a couple of times when I almost dropped out of the PhD program. I was literally calling home nearly every day, talking to my mom and dad, telling them that the experience was brutal—the isolation, self-doubt, lack of community, and the extremely cold weather. I was having a tough time academically and socially.

At one point my friend set me up with a job interview in Texas for an engineering position in semiconductors—if I got it, I would have to drop out of school. I got on a plane to go home for break. And on the flight home I had a moment of clarity. I reflected on the opportunity I had been given. I reflected on my faith in God, my faith in Christ. I thought about the people in that issue of *Ebony* magazine, all the engineers I had met along the way who said it was going to be tough. I thought, "Why am I doing this in the first place? How many young black men get this opportunity?"

My father told me that if anything in life is worth it, it's going to cost you. He said you're going to have to invest the time and that you can do all things through Christ. He also said that faith does not make things easy. It makes them possible.

I ended up deciding on that plane ride that I was going to

stay in school. When I arrived home, I told my friend that I wasn't coming to Texas to interview. I ended up going back to Cornell and finishing my degree. The year I graduated, 1999, I was the only African-American male in the United States to receive a PhD in nuclear science and engineering.

✦

Back when I was in college, I wrote down ten things I wanted to accomplish with my life on a piece of paper. One of them was to start a tutoring company because I wanted to give back to young people from my community by sharing what I had been blessed with in terms of my degrees, my knowledge, and my understanding of math and science.

After I graduated Cornell I got a job in Silicon Valley with Hewlett-Packard/Agilent Technologies, working on electronic chips used in wireless devices such as cell phones. While I was working there, I started a tutoring company called Xcel Education Services. I would get to work at Agilent at 6 A.M. so I could leave early and tutor kids around the Bay Area. Honestly, the money wasn't good, but I loved it. A lot of the kids struggled in math. There were kids in eighth and ninth grade who didn't know their fractions or multiplication tables. I was able to make a difference.

After I got laid off at HP, I decided to see where this tutoring business would take me. By 2003 I was doing it full-time, and giving speeches around the Bay Area, telling kids my story.

In 2007 I spoke at an event for SMASH Academy, a summer science, technology, engineering, and math (STEM) enrichment program for underrepresented high school students of color. I shared my whole story. I told them about my thesis, about how I worked in tech on chips and wireless systems that go in their cell phone. I told them about the list of goals I had written to myself in 1991 and how I wanted to give back. They

were blown away. A few months later SMASH hired me as their academic director. It was a significant pay cut—I knew there were undergraduates making more than me. But I had to bite the bullet.

These days I work as the president and chief education officer of the Level Playing Field Institute (LPFI), which is the parent company of SMASH Academy. Through SMASH Academy, I'm able to do for the next generation what so many mentors and teachers did for me—prepare students of color to pursue and graduate with a STEM degree.

Our mission at LPFI is eliminating barriers for students of color and fostering untapped talent by teaching them STEM— science, technology, engineering, and math. Right now only about 9 percent of the entire workforce in science and engineering is African-American or Latino according to the National Science Foundation. But the vast majority of jobs, now and in the future, are in STEM. If we want our young people to be not only consumers of technology, but also creators, we need to do more.

This lack of diversity is a national crisis—not just for the students of color, but also from a national security standpoint. We're becoming a majority-minority country, and if we're not training our nation's young people for the jobs of the future, we're going to get left behind.

Right now SMASH has four summer academies—Berkeley, Stanford, UCLA, and USC. We have an average of seventy students per site each year. The scholars are low-income, from communities of color, and have an aspiration to pursue a STEM degree in college. We also started a middle school program two years ago called SMASH Prep—for African-American males in sixth, seventh, and eighth grades.

Many of these scholars come from schools where they don't have access to resources or the academic rigor necessary

to make a successful transition to college. So we try to expose them to that rigor and that experience. They start the summer after ninth grade, and they take classes ranging from algebra 2 to calculus, engineering design, computer science, and public speaking. And they come back every year for three years. We ultimately want them to be ready to major in a STEM field when they get to college.

◆

I love doing what I'm doing—inspiring hope, using my story to encourage others. I've had my ups and downs academically just like a lot of our scholars, but I was able to stay focused on my goals and my aspirations.

We turn away about 80 percent of applicants every year, and it breaks my heart. I want to serve more students in a way that's sustainable and scalable. I believe LPFI can become the national model for preparing high school students of color for careers in STEM. I call it the Holy Grail, the "moon shot"—being able to be high-scale and high-impact. No one is there yet. I want to push us there.

LPFI is changing the narrative that the students from our community just want to play video games and sports. But that's just not the case. SMASH Academy doesn't even have to advertise—students love the program and go back to their schools and spread the word. The demand is high: build it and they will come.

Yusef Shakur

AGE: 42

TITLE: CEO of YBS Consulting; Author; Educator; Community Organizer; BMe Leader

COMMUNITY: Detroit, MI

Growing up, fighting was my sport.

I was not an easy child to raise. My mother faced all types of problems—mainly stress from raising three children by herself, dating abusive men, and being unemployed. I believe all these things led her to abuse alcohol. My mischievous behavior didn't help either. Simple whippings would become beatings. And all those beatings that she poured onto me, I poured onto other people.

By the time I was fifteen, living in Detroit's Zone 8, I was known as a fighter. I had been in and out of the youth home on numerous charges, and earned the respect of many of the OGs in my neighborhood. Some kids get their recognition from playing sports; I got mine from gangbanging.

I was out of control as a gangbanger. It got to the point that when the phone rang, my mother didn't know if it was going

to be that phone call—the police saying that I was killed or that I killed someone. So when I was fifteen, my mother saved me from myself—she made me a ward of the state and sent me away to a training school.

In training school, I only dealt with some of the surface problems I had. So, when I was released at age seventeen, I was really unprepared for the real world. After being home, working and going to school, my fantasy world soon crashed when one of my teachers asked me how I felt about going to college. I told him, "I would love to go to college!" I was eighteen then, and that was my first in-depth conversation about college. But when I went home to think more about that conversation, reality began to set in, and it was like facing a nightmare, because I knew I couldn't relate to college. I didn't know what to do, so in my panic mode I decided to kill myself. My mother found me after I'd taken a handful of pills, and she called 911.

I went back to fighting and hustling soon after being released from the hospital. In March of 1992, at age nineteen, I went to prison for assault with attempt to rob, with a sentence of five to fifteen years for a crime I did not commit.

✦

My first stop was a prison called MTU, a young dude's prison. It was always going down—it was like the club in prison. I would fit right in.

I made a name for myself by gangbanging, and operating something called the Sucker Store, where I would buy stuff from the commissary and resell it at a higher rate. Also, I was in and out of the hole for fighting. By my fifth time in solitary, I was lonely and homesick. I was starting to question my so-called friends. I decided to write a letter to my father.

My father and I had not had any communication in ten

years. He had gone to prison when I was eight, for armed robbery and attempted murder. Even as a kid, I never had a great relationship with him. At the time I first wrote to him, he had been in prison about nine years, and he didn't even know if I was dead or in prison.

In the letter I was trying to ask my father for help, but I didn't know how. So I ended up writing, "I'm in prison, I'll be out in 3 months, I ain't trying to get one of them 'I Told You So' speeches."

My father wrote back to me right away. The first thing he wrote was, "I would never give you one of those 'I Told You So' speeches. You made a mistake. The question is what you're going to do with that mistake."

He also included a P.S. at the end: "You misspelled *knowledge*, *religion*, and a few other words. You need to get a dictionary."

His letter took a lot of pressure off my shoulders. A lot of things he wrote went right over my head. But I did comprehend the warmth, the love, and the care he felt for me.

We began to correspond regularly. I started to look forward to those letters. Whenever a letter came, I would stop whatever I was doing, go to my room, close the door, and dissect it.

My father's letters represented the first time in my life that I was consistently hearing positive words from a Black man. His words painted a picture in my mind of the person that I could become. He made me realize that if I had died at twenty, my legacy would have been as a gangbanger—nothing more. I felt worthless, and began to rebuild myself from the inside out with my father's guidance.

◆

In March of 1993, I was notified that I was being transferred to Alger prison. I was in shock because that was the prison where my father was housed. It was a maximum security facility. As

soon as I got there, I asked about my father. One guard told me he knew him: "He's an excellent prisoner."

As soon as I could, I went to the law library, where my father was working. We talked as much as we could until the time came to head back to our units. My housing unit was first, and we walked as slowly as we could, deep in conversation the whole way. When we arrived at my unit my father hugged me and said: "The greatest gift that a father can give his child is precious time. Up to this point, I've neglected you in giving you my time. But from this point on I will do everything in my power to give you my time."

My father loved me back to life and off the deathbed of being a gangbanger. I started to follow his direct example. He had changed his name to Ahjamu Baruti, so I changed my name to Yusef Bunchy Shakur. He was eating healthy, so I learned how to eat well and exercise. He wasn't trying to shove these things down my throat; he just created a framework for me to step into. He became a beautiful example of what a Black man should be.

I was transferred out of Alger after six months. I kept building myself up in my father's framework. I started devouring books about Black history—George Jackson, Bunchy Carter, Malcolm X, and Assata Shakur. I met other guys that had the same desire for knowledge and self-transformation. Guys like Shaka Senghor. We transformed our prison experience into a sort of college, where we became professors to each other. Our friendship was built on the love of growth, of challenging each other to be better.

My father helped me change my thought process so I wouldn't see the world through the eyes of a thug, but through the eyes of a human being. That demanded that I behave like a human being. See, prison didn't rehabilitate me—my father did.

Five whole years went by before my father and I saw each

other in person again. By divine providence, I was transferred
to another prison, Carson City, he was at. Carson City was bro-
ken up into sections based upon levels. I was being transferred
to Level 2, but since I was close to earning a parole I knew there
was a high probability I would be transferred to Level 1 soon.

I visited my father in the library where he worked, and for a
couple of days we spent every possible moment together. A few
days in, when we heard my name come over the microphone,
we knew our time was up. My father escorted me to the gate
as I prepared to move to Level 1, and once we arrived there,
he looked at me with tears in his eyes and told me, "They can
keep the lion caged, but the cub must go free. And when the
cub goes free, part of the lion goes with him."

✦

I left prison on parole on January 31, 2001, after doing nine
years. My first two years on the outside were the hardest. Even
though I had come home a changed person, I was rejected by
society every step of the way and my support was close to zero.
I started working for different temp agencies and ultimately
got hired permanently as a Head Start teacher, which took me
back to my roots in activism and organizing that I developed in
prison. I published my first book, *The Window 2 My Soul*, and
began to work for myself as an author and speaker.

I ultimately opened a bookstore in my old neighborhood,
Detroit's Zone 8, which also operated as a community center.
In terms of culture, Zone 8 is a desert. It would have been so
easy to go open up a bookstore in midtown, where there is al-
ready culture and wealth. But it's all water in midtown. Up here
in Zone 8, people need the rain.

When we think of "undeveloped" places, we tend to think
about third world countries. But here in Detroit we've got third
world neighborhoods. We've got a third world city, producing

undeveloped human beings who are caught up in the suspense of undevelopedness. These communities don't have the nurturing influence of families, of strong businesses or strong churches. The mentality of the streets is filling those voids. But the mentality of the streets is lacking love, "overstanding," and caring. So the undeveloped man becomes a beast. He becomes a savage.

When I would get into fights as a child, it was a direct result of this undeveloped love. I didn't have the love of my father, or the love of my community. So I would seek recognition from the OGs who ran the streets.

The great equalizer that needs to come back in our community is love and hope. Poverty has never been an excuse to behave poorly, but without love and hope, poverty becomes overwhelming. When love walked out the door, hope left, peace left, violence walked right in.

✦

One Father's Day recently, my eight-year-old son called me. He said, "I want a job. I want to start cutting grass. I don't even know where to start from." So for Father's Day I got up and took him out. I showed him how to cut the grass. And he's a little guy. He was wrestling with that lawn mower. But he got it. He figured out how to do it.

Being able to instill in him a work ethic—that's incredibly important. These days I feel the need to be a father—not only for my son, but for my whole community. I need to be that person that brings love and provides the same example my father provided for me in prison.

In Zone 8, I started an organization called Restoring the Neighbor Back to the Hood, Inc. We want to create a neighborhood model that can be duplicated across the country.

Every year we host an annual school supply event at my

mom's house. It's a block party and we give away free backpacks filled with school supplies. My homeboys who sell dope and gangbang will stop selling dope and banging on that day. They may not have spent any time with their children all year long, but on that day they're with their kids. Despite the ugliness, we brought some beauty to the neighborhood.

We all have our own individuality, but it has to be tied into a collective responsibility. For Black folks, caring and loving is our tradition. Our caring and loving brought us through slavery; it brought us through fighting the Ku Klux Klan. The act of caring and loving can bring us back together and rebuild our communities.

In the hood, we want change. We're just tired of being excluded from the process. So that's the importance of a Yusef, being able to talk about that. These days when I talk about fighting, I mean fighting the good fight, the fight to restore the neighbor back to the hood.

Van Jones

AGE: 46

TITLE: Activist; TV Host; Author

COMMUNITY: Oakland, CA; Washington, DC; Los Angeles, CA

I've always been a renegade nerd.

I've never had a beer. I've never smoked a cigarette. Never tried any drugs. Because alcoholism runs strong on my dad's side of the family, I decided early on to stay clear of any intoxicants.

I grew up on the edge of a small town in rural western Tennessee. My father was born in poverty and segregation in Memphis. He joined the military, put himself through college, helped his brother and cousin go to college; he was a serious boot-strapper kind of guy. He was one of the first African-Americans to run a middle school in my hometown. They gave him the worst school in the county. He turned it into the best.

My mother was born in high-class black society. Her father was a PhD and a college president. Her extended family boasted preachers, teachers, beauticians, and morticians—the

four pillars of the black middle class in the South. So my mom grew up in the bougie part of the black community.

I was born in 1968, so schools were still in the later processes of trying to make desegregation work. The kids would go into the same school building together and sit in the same class. But the advanced kids, i.e., the white kids, sat on one side, and the remedial kids, i.e., the black kids, sat on the other side. The building was integrated but the classrooms were still segregated inside.

✦

I was a bully magnet. I was a geek who read comic books and wrote angst-ridden poetry and drew cartoons. I even had a Jheri curl. In junior high school, I would get my lunch, and I would take it out of the cafeteria, down the hall, and into the gym, which was of course empty and dark. I would sit behind the bleachers and eat by myself.

My mom told me something that made a huge difference for me. She said, "For some kids, high school is the peak of their lives. They are the class president, quarterback, cheerleading captain. And for the rest of their lives, they're going to look back and talk about high school, because that's their peak. This is not your peak."

✦

I graduated from high school in 1986 and went to the University of Tennessee at Martin. I decided to start fresh. My first day on campus I sat in the parking lot, and I said to myself: "I've got to plan this out, man. First of all my name is Anthony Jones. This is not a good name. Everybody who is cool has a one-syllable name, so I've gotta come up with one." So I thought maybe I should be Rush Jones, Jet Jones . . . and I landed on "Van Jones." I hit the dorm and told people my name was Van. I've been Van Jones ever since.

Soon enough I was trying to take the campus over. I started running for things—vice president of my dorm, then president of my dorm. Soon my friends and I took over the student government and then the student newspaper. I also started my own underground newspaper. I loved the whole philosophy of journalism, the idea that you can go anywhere, ask any question, and hold people accountable.

✦

I was constantly starting shit, constantly attacking the administration over anything I could. In the 1980s AIDS had just become a big deal, so my friends and I led an effort to put condom vending machines in the dorms. Now, this was in the buckle of the Bible belt in the middle of the Reagan-Bush era. We had a ballot measure put in the next campus elections and had students vote for it. We had a protest. My dad saw me on TV and he was like, "Of all the things that you could be marching for, you're gonna be marching for rubbers?" He was appalled.

Eventually I decided I wanted to go to law school. I was going because the struggle wasn't over; because of all the racism I saw. If I could have gone to any political training school, or if I could have gone overseas to some third world country and learned how to be a freedom fighter, I probably would have done that too. All I could think up at that time, though, was go to law school. So I ended up at Yale Law.

✦

In law school I wasn't just an activist; I was a militant. If I thought someone was being racist, I would verbally attack at any time—with no grace or mercy.

Then, I met a white woman named Dottie Zellner. She worked at the Center for Constitutional Rights in New York City, where I was an intern in the summer of 1991. She had

worked with the Student Nonviolent Coordinating Committee (SNCC) during the Civil Rights era. Dottie took me under her wing. I had been a black nationalist—fascinated by Malcolm X and the Black Panther Party. But she taught me about SNCC and how the white kids and black kids had worked together to change the country. She told me, "If it can happen once, it can happen again."

I came out of law school in 1993 with crazy hair and crazy ideas. I moved to the Bay Area to work as a fellow for the Lawyers' Committee for Civil Rights. I befriended radicals and anarchists and communists and every kind of "ist" I could find. They were every color in the rainbow—Latinos, Samoans, Koreans, Native Americans, African-Americans, you name it.

After a few months, the public interest law firm was fed up with me. I was too difficult. At every staff meeting, I would talk about revolution, how our organization was selling out, that kind of thing.

The firm's executive director, Eva Paterson, saw through all of my rhetoric and posturing—and she believed I still had potential. So she moved me off of her payroll, but she gave me a different kind of shot. She gave me a big closet in the back of her office complex, to use as my "office" for a project that I could run on my own. I had some fellowship money, plus the help of two other young lawyers. We took the shelves out of the closet; we put in a desk from home. We dragged in an extension cord, so I could plug in my Macintosh SE/30. That is where, in 1996, I cofounded the Ella Baker Center for Human Rights.

The thing that pissed us off at the Ella Baker Center the most was the prison industrial complex. We built a computer database to track unlawful police activity, and created a hotline, Bay Area Police Watch, for local people to call about police issues. Our tactics worked. By the mid-2000s, we had turned a closet-size operation in the back of a law firm into a community

institution with multiple programs that filled two stories. We were reliable to the point where, if the cops shot somebody, people didn't ask what the ACLU thought about it. They thought, "What does the Ella Baker Center think about it?"

✦

But I was already in the late stages of severe burnout. So many police killings, so many protests, so many funerals. I was emotionally exhausted, physically exhausted, spiritually exhausted. I was making a lot of mistakes in my personal life. I suddenly realized that I'd been in the Bay Area maybe a decade. But I didn't know where anything was—unless it had something to do with political activism. Like, where was the movie theater? Where was the ballpark? I had no idea.

I realized I needed to get healthy. I started going to retreat centers in Marin County. I learned about meditation and Buddhism. I met people who were not a part of this war I was fighting at all, and didn't know anything about it.

I started meeting people who were socially responsible entrepreneurs. I met people who ran companies in the solar industry, the wind industry, or green products. I started thinking, "Why don't we have these kinds of businesses in our community, and these kinds of jobs?"

And I got this idea in my mind, "green jobs, not jails." Because if we had green jobs, not jails, that would solve environmental, social, criminal justice, and economic problems. When Al Gore spoke about the environment, he got the problem statement right. But the full impact of the solution statement— more work, more wealth, and better health for people who needed all three—wasn't always there in a powerful way. So I began promoting a solution that could include everybody. You want solar panels? Let kids from the community put 'em up. Let's fight pollution and poverty at the same time.

I became an evangelist for this idea. Nobody believed in it, at first. Everybody thought I was crazy—including my own staff and board. My staff at the Ella Baker Center would literally laugh in my face, and *I* was the one signing their paychecks.

My board told me, "Shut this project down. This doesn't make any sense. It's mission creep. This has nothing to do with prisons. This has nothing to do with the criminal justice system. This is a criminal justice organization! What are you doing?"

I told them if they believed that, they could find someone else to run the organization. They didn't. And we soon spun off Green For All, which passed the Green Jobs Act of 2007 and has since helped to create more than ten thousand green jobs in more than fifty US cities.

◆

What I'm doing these days goes beyond reacting against racism and oppression. That only gets you so far. There's a power in a positive declaration. There's a power in possibility, in naming a future that you want and working for that.

Black politics in particular and progressive politics in general have become a politics of nostalgia and lament. It's all about missing the 1960s, missing Dr. King, and lamenting about either a bunch of bad stuff that happened in the past or bad statistics right now. That's it.

My view is, you're never, ever, ever going to move the country with that. You move the country when you say, here's a future that I want to fight for. Will you help me get us to this future? Can we build this future together?

I know this country better now than I did two decades ago. If someone says I want one billion dollars to fix the past—say, seeking reparations for slavery—nobody is moved. Nothing happens. If someone says they want one billion dollars to fix the present—say, to bring about some kind of redistribution of

wealth—nobody is moved. Nothing happens. But when someone says, I want a billion dollars to make a better future for all of our children—people are moved. Things begin to happen. People are happy to say, "Yes."

It's the same billion dollars. But anyone who is trying to make a better future for your kids and my kids, that person will get a different response.

I've been lucky to have built a lot of stuff—the Ella Baker Center, Green For All—to have helped to get Color of Change started, Rebuild the Dream, the #YesWeCode initiative, a lot of campaigns and fights along the way. Some worked; some didn't.

But what I have discovered at the end of the day is that the healthier I am inside myself, the better my ideas are and the easier it is for me to manifest them. Right now I'm trying to be at a place where I am well managed enough that I can build functional teams faster. If I can build them faster, generate ideas faster, then I can have those ideas become institutions faster.

I think about black folks coming out of our enslavement. Many didn't know how to read or write. That didn't stop them from building black churches that still stand to this day. That didn't stop them from building black colleges that produced Dr. King, Thurgood Marshall, Eleanor Holmes Norton. Our ancestors, under much worse circumstances, built world-class institutions that produced people who changed the course of history.

The institutions that we need to build today should be just as ambitious. We need to produce people who can change the world. If our forebears could do it with no money—while getting lynched and hounded by racist cops and having dogs sicced on them—well, you know, we can build good stuff in the face of the occasional mean Tweet.

Senator Rodney Ellis

AGE: 60

TITLE: State Senator, Texas 13th District

COMMUNITY: Houston, TX

I've now been in the Texas State Senate for twenty-five years. I've never had a Democratic challenger. I'd like to think it's because I've done a pretty good job. Or maybe it's because nobody wants the job.

I grew up on the southeast side of Houston, a low-income, African-American community called Sunnyside. My dad was a yardman and a nurse's aide by night, working the graveyard shift. Then he would come home to sleep, wake up around noon, and mow lawns in Houston's affluent neighborhoods during the hottest part of the day. We rarely had dinner together. My mother was a nurse's assistant. So my work ethic came from those two very strong black role models.

I'm a product of public schools. In high school I was the student body president in 1971–72, I was on the debate team, I was even on the slide rule team, if you can believe it. I was in high

school at the time that the Voting Rights Act forced Texas to change to single-member districts to elect members of the state legislature, which made the system fairer for black voters. So you had black politicians like Mickey Leland and Craig Washington winning seats in the state legislature. It was an exciting time.

I started volunteering on campaigns. Senior year on my prom night, instead of getting into some type of trouble like a lot of my friends, I was out hanging up signs for people who were running for state rep and lieutenant governor. That was my introduction to politics.

When I graduated high school I went to Xavier in New Orleans for a year. I went because my principal wanted me to go. He thought I had the gift of gab, and he said, "I know you're Baptist, but you need to go over there where the nuns won't give a hoot about your smiling and slapping them on the back."

After a year I transferred to Texas Southern University. At Texas Southern I worked as assistant director of promotions and development for the athletic department. My job was to tutor the athletes and do promotions, so I got to know most of the black and Hispanic elected leadership in Houston up close.

I went to Austin to get my master's and then my law degree. While I was in law school I was also working at the state capitol for Bill Hobby, who I had campaigned for. They discouraged you from working, but I'd wear my jeans to class and then change clothes in my lime-green Volkswagen in the garage of the Capitol, put my suit on, and run into work.

✦

Not long after law school, Mickey Leland offered me a job to go to Washington and become chief of staff for his congressional office. Mickey was my mentor. He had been an antipoverty activist who won a seat in the Texas House of Representatives when the election process changed. In 1979 he was elected to

Congress. I'd been out of law school maybe two years. I was twenty-four years old. And I went to Washington as the chief of staff and roommate to a junior member of the United States Congress.

✦

A few years later, with Mickey's blessing, I ran for Houston City Council, and at twenty-nine years old, I became the second-youngest person in the history of the council at the time.

As an aside, I was scheduled to be with Mickey on the trip to Ethiopia when his plane crashed. His chief of staff called me about five days before the trip and told me there were not enough women on the trip, so I was being bumped. I remember having harsh words with her, because I'd been planning to go. As fate would have it, my number was not up.

After the crash I tried to get Mickey's widow to run for his congressional seat, and she was trying to get me to run. I just couldn't—emotionally, I couldn't take it. I backed Craig Washington, a state senator and another very close ally. He won, and I decided to throw my hat in the ring to take his Senate seat. I've been in the state Senate ever since.

✦

I treat my Senate office as a mini civil rights organization.

The Texas legislature meets 140 days every other year, so it is a game for the swift. My dad used to say, "If you want to get something done, find somebody who's busy." And in some ways I deal with attention deficit disorder every day. But I'm best when I'm juggling four or five things at the same time. When you look through the six hundred or so bills that my staff and I have been the lead author on, we're all over the board—from the largest state-funded student financial aid program in the history of Texas, to the CHIP expansion that is the gold stan-

dard for health care on a state level. We've been pretty good policy wonks.

I don't want criminal justice to define me, but I'm very proud of the work I've done around the issue. I'm not sure why I have such a passion for criminal justice. Sometimes if you want to look for light, you go to where there's darkness. And there's just so much darkness in terms of the criminal justice system in Texas. There are such a large number of people, disproportionately African-American, overwhelmingly poor, who end up in the system.

You know, I was arrested back in junior high school. I was on the bus, on the way back from school. Some black kids from my school were being thuggish, tearing up the bus. The driver got off the bus and announced he was going to a pay phone to call the police. So the kids who were tearing up the bus all got off.

Now, it was hot as hell. I wasn't about to walk the two miles home. And my logic said that if I got off the bus, it would indicate that I was guilty of something. Anyway, the police finally arrived. Obviously, the bus driver was white. The police officers were white. All the people on the bus in that neighborhood were African-American. And there were about five young black boys on the bus, including me. I figured, "Surely, I'm okay." I had my student council badge on. Instead of a knife, I had a slide rule. But the police came on the bus and they took three of us black boys into the back of their police car and brought us downtown. They eventually dropped the charges, but I never forgot that, the unfairness of it.

When I got in a position where I could impact the criminal justice system, I wanted to do it. I've been able to get the Fair Defense Act passed, which clarified the right to counsel. I've helped increase the compensation for people who have been wrongfully convicted. I've passed stronger DNA testing laws, and done good work with the Innocence Project as well.

✦

I was mentored. I had the good fortune of volunteering as an intern, which led to paying jobs, and it helped make me the serious policy wonk that I am today. In a lot of ways, I was groomed for the position I hold today.

I've created an internship program patterned after one that Mickey Leland had me do when I worked for him. He had a program called the Leland Internship Program, where he took ten college students from his district to Washington to work in other members' offices as a way of diversifying their staffs and his staff. I started that on the state level when I went to the state Senate in 1990, and I called it the Texas Legislative Internship Program (TLIP).

I had five students for the first session in 1991. This past session, I had sixty-seven students. I had to raise close to a half million dollars. I bring them in from universities in Texas, Louisiana, around the country, some international students. I place them in legislative and advocacy offices around the Senate. They get academic credit, and I give them a stipend of $7,000 each.

The TLIP is something I'm very proud of. There are now three members of the statehouse—one black, two Hispanic— who the first time they walked into the state capitol, they were in my program. Another alumnus was appointed to a judgeship in Jefferson County, and most are successful role models.

✦

As far as leadership development, there's a real challenge in our country: a lot of people are turned off by politics. They have a total disdain for it.

I always have to explain to young people that politics is in everything you do. My internship program is just a small dent into the larger problem. We've got to get more of these

young African-American males and females, Hispanics, Native Americans, people who are gay and lesbian, we have to get them hooked on politics, excited about politics, and not always waiting for an inspirational candidate. I mean there are only so many Barack Obamas out there. We've got to encourage more of these people to go out and make themselves the heroes and heroines.

My greatest hope is that if down the road I'm still putting my name on the ballot and I lose this Senate seat, it will be one of these young people that I've mentored who will take me out and keep moving us forward.

Alex Peay

AGE: 27

TITLE: Social Innovator; Founder, Rising Sons; BMe Leader

COMMUNITY: Philadelphia, PA

During my sophomore year at Ursinus College, there was a racial incident on my campus. Ursinus is a mostly white school near Philadelphia. One night some lacrosse players got drunk and took pictures of each other with derogatory words and images on their bodies like swastikas and "whore"; one guy drew whiplashes on his back. They posted the pictures on Facebook, and there was a big uproar.

I decided to start a discussion group with some other black men on campus. We started out small, just a few of my friends talking about the incident and how black students could mobilize around civil rights issues. But we found that there were no other support groups for black men on campus, and soon enough we were growing in numbers.

We went from five to fifteen members in a year's time. We started something called "Get Fresh Friday," when we would

dress professionally and eat dinner together. So if you can imagine, like, fifteen black men coming to the cafeteria, dressed . . . no hootin' and hollerin', no steppin', chantin', no nothin'. That silence caused an uproar. People were like, "What are these guys doing? Are they coming from court or something?" But it was just us eating dinner. This was the birth of Rising Sons.

Rising Sons has evolved in so many different capacities over the years. We started doing service initiatives—Family Day cookouts, feeding the homeless, giving holiday toys to kids in poor neighborhoods. After I graduated in 2009, we moved the program to Philadelphia, where I'm running it full-time. More than anything, we're a family. We all look out for each other. We say to each other all the time, "Hey family, what's going on? Hey Rising Sons family, what's going on?" I want my kids to call the other members Auntie and Uncle.

I'm probably so family-oriented because I had a close family growing up, but then I lost it all.

✦

I was blessed to have both parents in my life when I was young. It was a very loving, very caring environment. My father always told me and my two brothers that education comes first, and my mother was always there with love.

Then everything changed—quickly. My dad left the house one day when I was twelve years old—he said he was going to visit my grandmother, but then he just disappeared. So my mother was left to raise us alone. Then a few months later, my mother got arrested. She was a public school teacher, and she was caught having an affair with one of her students. It hit the news all over Maryland. The state called Child Protective Services, and my dad came back to pick us up.

We left Maryland that same day and moved in with my aunts in New York. It was ten of us living in this small house

in Queens—me, my dad and brothers, my cousins, my grand-mother, and my aunts.

It was a lot to adjust to. I was barely thirteen. In the blink of an eye I had lost my mother, lost my home, and moved to a whole new city. I was forced to make new friends and learn how to be cool. Everything was new—from the New York City fashion to the general way of life there.

At first it seemed like my dad was going to be there again for me and my brothers. He would say, "I love you no matter what, I'm always gonna be here for you." But soon enough he met a woman from Brooklyn and disappeared for a few months. My aunt told me we might get evicted because he wasn't paying the bills.

Eventually he got back in touch with us, and we ended up moving in with him and his girlfriend in Brooklyn. But it was too late; there had been too many betrayals. He would tell us he loved us, but I didn't feel the love.

✦

I wasn't getting the support I needed at home, so I looked else-where. Freshman year of high school, I joined a gang, the "Baby Crips." A lot of the other guys were like me—they came from broken families, and they weren't getting enough love at home. So they would look to the streets. Being in a gang makes you feel like you're part of something.

I was never the kind that liked to fight out of anger, but I just needed to release it—I had a lot on my mind. So when it came time to fight other gangs, I was ready. But I didn't get a chance. Whenever we were getting ready to head out to meet the other gang, the guys would stop me and say, "Where do you think you're going?" I was like, "I'm going with all of you." And they would say, "Nah, you stay here. You don't get involved with this stuff. Just keep doing what you're doing."

I would get really mad. I didn't understand why they didn't need me. It wasn't until I got older that I realized what they were doing. They noticed that I was trying to do something in my life—they saw something in me that even I didn't see. They were protecting me.

A lot of my inspiration for Rising Sons came from my experience with those guys. It upsets me that a lot of them—the same guys who looked out for me—they're locked up now, or dead, or still on the corners at night, doing the same thing. We look at these people and we say that they're destroying America, but they saved me.

◆

In between sophomore and junior year of high school I moved to Brooklyn with my dad. It was good timing: I was in a new neighborhood so I stopped hanging out with the Baby Crips and started going to church, started focusing more on school. Education became my defense mechanism and my support system.

When I was sixteen, my uncle Kenny, my father's brother, started teaching in my high school. He was a music teacher, and he quickly became well loved by everyone in school. I would go to his classroom during lunch and talk to him.

Whenever my dad wasn't there, Uncle Kenny stepped into the picture. He kept me motivated, kept me inspired. He taught me how to tie a tie, taught me the difference between a good handshake and a bad handshake—he called it a live fish versus a dead fish. He would give me a few nickels before I left so I could go get a healthy meal, because he knew I was not going to get one at home. There's no greater love than the love Uncle Kenny brought me through the years.

In his spare time, my uncle ran a youth group that empowered black boys through music—a gospel choir. A lot of the guys in that choir might have been in a gang if it wasn't

for him. He knew that, so he used some of the same tricks the gangs used—an initiation ceremony, a whole culture of little signs and signals.

Uncle Kenny passed away when I was nineteen, the summer before I started Rising Sons. I still cry about it, because during that time in my life I didn't have any other male mentors. Uncle Kenny's memory still lives on through the program. We also have our own signs and colors, our own handshakes and hand signals. They're all reminders that when you join Rising Sons, you belong to something—you have other people looking out for you.

✦

Senior year of college I was homecoming king and commencement speaker for the Ursinus Class of 2009. I spoke in front of three thousand people, most of them white. It was also one of the worst days of my life.

When the ceremony came around, my aunt and my godparents showed up, but none of my immediate family came to hear me speak. My dad showed up extra late and said to me, "Oh, I can get the ceremony on DVD." But it was not a DVD kind of moment.

After everything I'd gone through, I just wanted my family to be there. As I was walking back to my dorm, I ran into the dean of students, who I knew from Rising Sons. She saw how upset I was. She looked at me and she said, "Well, you know, Alex, your Ursinus family was here."

That's how I feel about Rising Sons, too. Even though I started the group, I'm a product of it as well. I have more confidence; I know I can do stuff. I'm not afraid of what's coming up, because I know I have a group of other young men and women to help me get to the next step. I know someone is there to say "I got you, it's gonna be all right."

That's what we do at Rising Sons—we motivate each other. We're all in the same boat. We have each other and that's what keeps us going. We all know it's not going to be easy, but as long as we stick by each other, and work together, one day, someone's going to see us.

I just think about this picture I once saw. This guy, he has a shovel and he keeps on digging and digging and digging and digging and the diamonds are right there. But he gives up after a couple of scoops. He could have had those diamonds but he gave up. You know, so I don't want to be like that. So we're just going to keep on digging, digging, digging, until we reach that diamond.

Lance Goodwin

AGE: 50

TITLE: President and Founder, Trucked Out SUV Club; Community Advocate

COMMUNITY: Brooklyn, NY

I hear folks say all the time, "I've heard of motorcycle clubs and auto clubs, but what's an SUV club?" For lack of a better term, it's a motorcycle club on four wheels.

Originally, I didn't know what an SUV club was either. Then, one night in 2004, I was hanging out with a group of guys in Brooklyn and we saw a truck club called Team Expo rolling in a convoy down Linden Boulevard. They were all in uniform, their trucks had the same markings, their rims were clean. There was an order—a discipline—to how they were rolling. They represented a cohesiveness that clicked for me. I wanted to create a similar sense of community with my group of guys.

It helped that so many of my friends already loved SUVs. We loved the sense of safety, power, and riding high that you get from an SUV. So we said, let's start our own club.

At the time, we didn't know anything about running a club, or that we might evolve into something that contributes to the community. We just thought it would be cool to ride together, in unison, fly our colors, so to speak, enjoy the bond and the brotherhood around a love of trucks.

We didn't create our club to do community service, but we found ourselves immersed in it—it focused us on a sense of purpose.

◆

Though I wouldn't have articulated it like this at the time, I started Trucked Out to extend the sense of community and belonging that I was born into and, admittedly, strayed from as a young adult.

I'm blessed to come from a loving, supportive family that embraces and embodies community, diversity, and inclusiveness. My father was black, and my mother was Japanese. They met and married in Japan, where he was stationed in the military. He brought her back to the United States, and they moved to South Carolina and then settled in Brooklyn. When my mother arrived in the United States, she had no family, barely spoke English. My grandmother adopted her, taught her to cook soul food, made her an honorary African-American.

Growing up, we weren't wealthy by any means, but we were comfortable, and I had both my mom and dad present at home. I was always a good student. I even skipped the eighth grade. When I finished high school, I bumped around a couple of jobs, first as a driver at a ladies' clothing factory, then as a forklift operator. But I was drawn to the hustle of the streets.

It was never that I needed the money—both my parents worked—but I was drawn to the celebrity of hustling. It's funny, my friend who hustled with me also came from a two-parent home; we both grew up with enough money, so to

say we did it because we came from broken homes—that's not an excuse for us. We just did it with no real reason at all.

And the funny thing about it is that we were really successful at it. But after a few months, a couple of friends and I were arrested for possession of cocaine and possession of a loaded firearm. I beat the cocaine charge, but they stuck me with the felony gun charge, and I did some time in the penitentiary.

Having my five- and seven-year-old children visit me in an environment that no kid should be exposed to really hit home. It made me think about the fact that this is not what I wanted for them. It was not what I wanted for myself, but I definitely didn't want it for them. I knew that as soon as I got out, I'd figure out a way to be a positive role model and better provider.

When I came home, it was hard to find work. Being a convicted felon without a college education—these are strikes against too many black men, and it made the path very difficult. I applied for so many jobs and took any test I could get my hands on, but no one ever called back. I'd been a good student in school and always did well on the tests, but it wasn't enough. I am very fortunate that I was eventually given a chance at Verizon, where I've worked for the past fifteen years.

✦

In the early days of Trucked Out, we'd gather on hot summer nights in Brownsville, Brooklyn, park our trucks in a row, and just hang out. A few of the guys had big sound systems, others had shiny rims. These showy elements weren't requirements, but guys take pride in their vehicles, invest their time and money in making them special. We liked the attention we generated.

In Brownsville in the summer, the kids are out in the street because it's too hot to stay indoors. So they started to take notice. They liked our SUVs and the fact that we were accessible,

welcoming, happy to talk to them and show them our vehicles. In a way, we were role models because we could afford these trucks through hard work at legitimate jobs. We would tell the kids as much. Furthermore, I'd done prison time for making choices that were about fast money and immediate gratification, and I'd dealt with the consequences of those choices, so I could communicate to the young folks. I had the credibility to offer a bit of "street ministry."

After a year or so, we looked at the way we could connect with the kids and started to realize that our club could have a higher purpose. We decided to use our club to help the kids in the neighborhood. Mind you, this was totally new territory for us. We had no idea how to go about it or what "helping out" actually even meant.

The first thing we started was a back-to-school giveaway. We gave away school bags with supplies—no small contribution in a community as poor as Brownsville. Eventually we started trying to do some sort of giveaway or drive for every holiday—Halloween parties, Thanksgiving turkeys, Christmas toy drives, Easter egg hunts.

Now, this sounds funny to me even as I say it, but we met with the local police precinct to let them know what we were doing. Believe it or not, this became a basis for a real relationship. It also opened other doors, to politicians, to police officials, to people involved in social work in the community—even to the US Marines. Part of my growth as president of the club was to learn how to work with these groups, how to build partnerships that could benefit the community and also our membership.

◆

Building community has been at the core of our work, but the club is also about strengthening our individual members. I hold myself and our members to a high standard. We run all

of our meetings according to *Robert's Rules*, so we are learning governance as we govern. We also have three main requirements that all members have to meet: you have to have a steady job—it can't be a street hustle—you have to be willing to do community service, and you have to be willing to attend all of our meetings.

We ask all members to act as if they are the president of the club, as if it were something they created and want to see grow. I say all the time, "You don't need to be an officer to initiate something. If you have something to bring to the table that helps the community, bring it. We'll find the time and the budget to make it happen. This is not my club. This is our club."

We also help each other out through difficult times. When members have lost jobs and can no longer pay their dues, we find ways for them to stay involved. And when people have family issues they have to deal with, we are there to be of support and remind them that the family and job come first.

For instance, I've been able to mobilize some of the relationships that I've made with politicians and other officials to help some of our members when they need a hand. I go to our leaders and say, "I've given you our support in the past, I've got a member that's not working right now but is qualified. Is there someone you know that might have a job they can apply for?"

✦

We've been in existence now for ten years. Many truck clubs have come and gone during that time, but this is something I want to leave to our kids. I want our kids to take it over and for them to continue doing our work until their kids can take it over. To this end, we have our own kids actively involved in the community work that we do. They are out there volunteering their time, helping out, serving food, giving away toys, painting faces.

My son and other members' sons work at the Marines' warehouse throughout December, helping to run the Toys for Tots program. During December, we're there every day. I ask our members to help out when they can. If they're working during the day, come at night. If they have vacation time saved up, use it then. I save a lot of my vacation time, and I take it to participate in the Toys for Tots program because it is an extremely busy time for the Marines. Chipping in when they need help is the least we can do.

So now when people ask me what an SUV club is, I've got this track record that I point to. We have the bond and the brotherhood that other clubs cultivate. We profile our convoys through Brownsville in uniform. We attend competitions and often bring home the trophies that the other clubs are there to win. But we also make contributions to the community. We inspire kids. We support the Marines in their volunteer efforts. We are a partner to officials and clergy in their efforts to connect with the community.

These contributions to the community are something our core members probably would not have done without the club. But I've found—and they've found—that once you get involved and you see the effect that it has, once you see the appreciative smiles that you get from some of these kids, it makes it all worth it. This is the legacy of Trucked Out. This is what we're building for the long run.

Isiah Thomas

AGE: 53

TITLE: Chairman & CEO, Isiah International; Founder, Mary's Court Foundation; NBA Hall of Famer

COMMUNITY: Chicago, IL; Detroit, MI; New York

There is the poverty line, and then there is the line that is below poverty. My family was classified below the poverty line. I grew up on the West Side of Chicago with six brothers and two sisters. My siblings and I joined the local basketball teams at Our Lady of Sorrows and the Boys and Girls Club because we knew those places had food. We knew that if you participated in sports, you got something to eat.

When I was in eighth grade I received a scholarship to play basketball at St. Joseph High School in Westchester, Illinois, a suburb of Chicago. Every morning I would leave my house at 4:30 A.M. for a two-and-a-half or three-hour trip out to Westchester. I would take the bus to the end of the line, then the train to the end of the line, and then I walked a mile and a half to school.

During the long commute to St. Joseph, I could see the

visual changes in the neighborhoods and communities. The farther I traveled from my neighborhood, the less poverty I noticed. In the suburbs, I would see bigger houses, greener grass. I rarely saw litter in the streets, or vacant lots or abandoned homes. I would always ask myself, why is there such a difference?

St. Joseph was where I learned how to code switch. I learned to adjust to different environments, to assimilate, and to articulate my viewpoints and communicate with people from different cultures and different socioeconomic backgrounds. This experience reaffirmed my belief in what my parents taught me at a young age: education is the great equalizer, and it is the gateway to success.

✦

Education was strongly emphasized in my household and community. We were taught that it was the best way for African-Americans to move forward in society. Even though we were on welfare, many times my mom would take the welfare check and, instead of buying food, she would make sure there were books in the house. It felt like education was more of a priority than food.

In my household, educators were held in the highest esteem: the people who could read and write, who had a command of the English language. They were our heroes and role models. They were the people my mom and older sister would encourage me to follow. It was such that the posters in my room growing up were not of NBA or NFL players—they were posters of Angela Davis, Malcolm X, and Dr. Martin Luther King Jr. The only sports poster I had was the one that my mother sent off to college with me: a poster of Cassius Clay, aka Muhammad Ali.

My mom was definitely the activist in the family. She worked

at the community center and cooked in the monastery for the nuns and priests. When Dr. Martin Luther King Jr. came to the West Side of Chicago, my mom was out there with him. When Fred Hampton was murdered, my mom made sure that we all went to the funeral. She taught us how to be activists—how to use our voices, how to march, and how to protest.

At the time I was coming up, gangs were just getting started in Chicago. Before they were considered "gangs," however, they were just community-based organizations that were actually rebuilding and reinvesting in the community. The first and original gang was the Vice Lords. My mom actually worked with them. She would help the kids recently released from prison get reacclimated to the community. Then, in the 1960s, drugs invaded the neighborhood. Heroin decimated the minds and bodies of many young black men. Parents were not unaware of the devastating effects of heroin, and they could not prevent their kids from using it. Many of our brothers and sisters fell victim to the deadly drug, and it corrupted organizations that were originally trying to help the community, not hurt it. It was a big change.

✦

For me, basketball was the ticket to go anywhere. The one thing about sports, particularly basketball at the time, was that there were no boundaries. When you had potential on the basketball court, there was no East Side, no West Side, no South Side, and no suburbs anymore. The game allowed you to go anywhere and to experience different people, different cultures, and different races.

My immediate mentors growing up were my parents and siblings, but I was also fortunate enough to have coaches who reinforced the values that were coming from home. One of my first coaches was John McLendon, a former student of Dr.

James Naismith, who coached me at the Dr. Martin Luther King Jr. Boys and Girls Club in Chicago. There was Gene Pingatore, my high school coach at St. Joseph, Bob Knight in college, and Chuck Daly in the NBA. All of these men are in the NBA Hall of Fame or their local Hall of Fame.

All of these men were values-based coaches who taught me about basketball from a philosophical level. They taught me that basketball is at heart about bringing people together. It's about figuring out how you fit on the team, and how you define your relationship with your teammates on the court and off. They were all from the Vince Lombardi school of thought: you build a man first, and the player will come after that.

I was blessed to have had a long career in the NBA, as a player, coach, broadcaster, and executive. However, I've always remembered that, growing up, our family business wasn't sports—it was activism. We were taught to give back to the community. Giving back as an adult was not a choice for me— it was the family business. When I achieved success, giving back came with the territory.

Whenever I talk about the issues facing black men today, I try to address them from the perspective of poverty. If you're not looking at poverty, employment, and the financial health of our communities, then you're overlooking the foundational problems. Poverty affects kids in a holistic way. One of the biggest issues impacting kids who live in poverty are failing schools. They hinder kids' ability to communicate effectively. Without the right vocabulary these kids become vulnerable, because they can't articulate their problems. Then the door is opened for someone else to define their problems for them.

Poverty also affects kids' health—kids are growing up hungry and living in communities where "food deserts" are the norm. As a result, kids are eating foods that don't provide the proper nutrients to grow physically or mentally.

✦

One of the things that really bothers me is that the kids who are going to failing schools and living in food deserts must also contend with recreation and sports programs being budgeted out of their community. Park districts are closing down; recess and physical education classes are being cut from schools. For many of these kids, the only way they can play a sport is if they make a team. That means that only fifteen or twenty kids in a community are going to be able to participate in a particular sport.

This is why I helped start the PEACE Games. In 2011, I joined Father Michael Pfleger of St. Sabina Church in Chicago on his weekly community walk on the South Side of Chicago. As we walked the streets, young men and women were coming from everywhere to greet us. As we talked to the young people and some of the community leaders, I would ask this question: If Father Pfleger and I brought you together for a game of basketball promoting peace, would you show up? The immediate response was yes. We wanted to give the young men a chance to get to know one another on and off the court. If we could bring them together, along with the community, around a game of basketball, we knew we had a chance to break down some of the territorial barriers that had been created.

The first year of the PEACE Games, we bused the kids in from each neighborhood separately because they were worried they would get hurt if they were found in hostile territory. Now, those kids are more comfortable attending the games together. The commitment and involvement from the players and the whole community around the PEACE Games is really powerful. What was just a small idea has now grown into peaceful basketball tournament. More importantly, the young men who compete are offered life-skills classes, mentoring, GED classes, employment training, and other opportunities.

Earning respect, having a positive reputation, and being a valued member of a group or a team are concepts that are some of the reasons I am where I am today. It is important for our young people to know that respect is given and never taken, and that a worthwhile reputation comes from doing honest work and not hard time. They need to know the only group worth being a part of requires giving back through teamwork.

When you take sports and recreation out of the community, people do not have an opportunity to get to know one another. If you do not make the effort to know a person, you might be a little suspicious of that person. You might create myths, stories, and lies about that person. This is why, with the PEACE Games, we bring people together. When you bring people together and they get to know each other, things start to get a little better.

Travis McCready

AGE: 45

TITLE: Vice President for Programs, the Boston Foundation; Founder, SoulyOwned, LLC

COMMUNITY: New York, NY

I have come to appreciate that I am one complicated dude. I've also come to appreciate the fact that I am a contradiction in many ways. I'm a former athlete, a former artist. I'm someone who has been privileged to know some extraordinary people in this world, who has had the opportunity to be pushed and challenged by them. I am very much spiritual, though not religious. I'm trying to be a better Buddhist, but I've got a ways to go.

But more than anything, amidst all those contradictions, my overall conclusion is that I am Black.

The older I get, the more I understand that there's a richness to our cultural heritage, which has its own built-in contradictions. In many ways, our Blackness makes each and every one of us an iconoclast. And I embrace that identity.

✦

I am very much my mother's son. My mom was perhaps an even more complicated person than myself.

My mother's side of the family came from the South. She grew up in Brooklyn, next to a Hasidic Jewish community, and my grandfather followed the teachings of the Moorish Science Temple. Between the Jewish community and the Temple, she held education in highest esteem and an unapologetic belief in self-empowerment.

My parents divorced when I was two, so my mother raised me and my three brothers herself. My mother intended for us all to be great. She didn't specify what we had to be great at, but it had to be something. She truly believed—and she brainwashed me to believe—that there was no power greater than the power of our dreams and of the human spirit. She never placed any limitations on us, whatsoever.

Mind you, she beat the living snot out of us if we disrespected her or popped off at the mouth. But this woman was very deliberate in her beatings. Here's a classic example. One day I took one of my older brother's chemistry kits and I got it in my head to mix all the chemicals together in a single test tube. So I placed my thumb over the test tube and shook it. I don't know what was in the damn tube, but the pressure pushed my thumb off the tube and this brown goo exploded all over the walls in our white-painted bedroom. I destroyed bedsheets, walls—I caused some damage.

Now, this was in East Flatbush, Brooklyn. We were growing up on public assistance, and as my mother used to say, we didn't have two nickels to rub together. So when my mother came home from work I was terrified. But when she saw what had happened, she told me she was proud of me for experimenting. She asked me to catalog the chemicals that I had mixed together in the tube.

To me, that just epitomizes my mother's approach. She was

damned tough, but she was also very strategic about her tough-ness. It was never designed to break us down; it was always designed to lift us up.

✦

A couple years before my mother died, I asked her why she had never remarried. Her response was "I didn't want another man coming up in my house, and ruining my program."

To be sure, the "program" was challenged a number of times. When I was in junior high school my best friend was named Fred. We went to this extraordinary private school in Brooklyn Heights called Saint Ann's. It was very alternative for its day—there were no grades; it was all about exploration, self-actualization.

When I was thirteen, a good friend started getting mixed up in using and selling drugs, vandalism, being defiant toward his mother, the works. I could very easily have gotten sucked into that world . . . the friend and I were close. But I went to my mother to talk about it, and on her advice I ended up cutting ties with him. It wasn't easy—again, we were close—but it was necessary. Besides, I also knew that if I didn't, she would have killed me.

The second time my mother's program was challenged was when I started playing for the Riverside Church basketball team, one of the most prestigious AAU programs in the city. When I rolled up into the church for the first day of practice, it was one of the very first moments I deeply understood the concept of code-switching, of being multilingual in the Black community. I was around fourteen or fifteen years old, and I had spent virtually my entire lifetime going to private schools and being around my family, none of whom have a Brooklyn accent or a New York accent. I spoke very clearly, very articu-lately; I didn't cuss and frankly thought that that was normal.

The dudes on the team didn't get me, and they teased me and razzed me about everything—but what they said about the way I spoke hurt the most. I remember coming home from practice and my head was all messed up. I desperately wanted to fit in. I sat down with my mother and told her all about it, and she basically laid the situation out. She said, listen, you have a couple of choices. You can learn to code-switch. You can quit the team. Or you can start running with these guys, and I will kill you. Nothing like clear choices. I chose to code-switch—one language at home, a different language at practice.

✦

Today I work as vice president for programs for the Boston Foundation, one of the oldest and largest community foundations in the nation. We coordinate grants to nonprofit organizations and work closely with nonprofits and community organizations in the Greater Boston area. Through our donors' generosity, we award $80 million to $90 million in grants annually to nonprofit organizations helping to make sure Greater Boston residents are successful and thriving, and our communities are vibrant and equitable. I oversee the entire grant-making strategy, which includes education, health and wellness, arts and culture, neighborhood vitality, and economic development. Though I am a system thinker—everything is connected—my passion and focus are for economic development, particularly ensuring that we have a robust and growing minority small business community. The reason is very simple—success of minority business leads to more jobs, which leads to more community benefits and in turn more positive social outcomes.

Through my work I keep meeting people who put forward this idea that we are in a postracial society. The presumption is that race isn't important, that it's a false construct. Frankly, I think that's bullshit.

What I find missing from the conversation is a discussion of positive narratives about Blackness and Black identity. I think it's a problem of Black people no longer having the confidence or the license to talk about it. It isn't part of the common lexicon for young people, taught actively (and passively) year round, in our homes, in our schools. And not just the same ol' stories either that we dust off and Disney-fy.

I remember early in my tenure at the foundation I offered to buy out a movie theater showing the Angela Davis documentary *Free Angela* and provide the tickets free of charge to a few community groups. Imagine my surprise when the response to my offer was met with "Who's Angela Davis?" Yeah, we're not lifting up and educating positive narratives about the Black experience.

I find it fascinating, instructive, and inspiring when, working in philanthropy, every time I sit down with someone who is Jewish, they will tell me that they are Jewish in at least three or five different ways throughout the conversation. And they'll always use very positive language about their Jewish identity. They'll talk about the experiences they've had with their rabbi, about how they have to prepare for the Seder coming up, or the great program at their synagogue that night . . . you name it.

So a couple of years ago, I decided that I would start doing the same thing. It's obvious that I'm Black, but now every time I talk to somebody or give a speech, I weave into the narrative some positive references to my Black identity. Real casual-like.

I just did it this morning, actually. I met this guy who is an executive director of an international organization. We got to talking about the Ethiopian community in Boston, and he mentioned how there were so many Ethiopian gentlemen working for parking companies. I used that opening to launch into a story about how one of these Ethiopian gentlemen had recently asked me where I was from, and I told him New York. His response was "No, no, man—where are you *from*?"

It was an emotional moment, as it would be for any Black American who knows the answer is America, knows that through our blood, sweat, ingenuity, and faith we all but built this country, but at the same time longs to know his African heritage. So I told the executive director all of this, and then just moved on to the next topic. I left him with that kernel. I think this whole concept of a postracial America doesn't allow for that kind of conversation to happen. It doesn't allow us to positively weave and integrate ourselves and our stories into the American narrative. I do very much believe that Black folks need to inject a more nutritious narrative into everyday conversation. We are each a product unto ourselves. So why not shape the narrative to the one you want it to be?

I think being able to connect to your identity, to your family, to your heritage—even just to your parents—it all communicates a certain peace and energy and power that I find to be very quieting. It provides resilience in what can be a hostile environment.

◆

People sometimes call American culture hostile to Black people, and there are some days I think they have a point. But I'm not about to get angry about it. It just is. At the same time, I think there are ways to make it less hostile, and we have control over that. It's not through public policy or legislation, and it's not through philanthropy, quite frankly. It starts with just being able to be quiet. Being able to understand our context, understand our history, understand our narrative, and understand that frankly, we've been here before. We have struggled before, overcome insurmountable obstacles, demonstrated ingenuity and innovation, and, more than anything else, demonstrated resilience and greatness. That's what we do, and in that we are unstoppable.

Rodney D. Foxworth Jr.

AGE: 30

TITLE: Deputy Director, Warnock Foundation

COMMUNITY: Northwest Baltimore, MD

Martin Luther King said the arc of history bends toward justice, but I would add a caveat to that: without empathy, there can be no justice.

I've found that empathy comes from connectivity with one another. When we are connected, when we feel empathy toward one another, we can all strive for justice together.

This sense of justice through empathy and connectivity started for me early. My mom worked at the Clarence Mitchell Courthouse in Baltimore for thirty years. From time to time, she would take me to sit at the courthouse and observe the proceedings. There'd be a line of thirty-five black boys, more or less my age, in handcuffs waiting to be sent to jail.

The experience had a profound impression on me. It made me ask questions. Is this really only the fault of the black boys? What are the conditions that have brought us here—not just

blacks, but our society as a whole? What can I do to contribute positively to society, to help reduce the line of young black males at the courthouse?

✦

I was fortunate to grow up in a household with two loving parents, my mom and my stepdad, and twin younger sisters. My stepdad raised me as his own son and I don't think of him as anything but my dad. He always had two or three physically demanding jobs to help support our family. My mom worked at the courthouse as a court clerk with the criminal division. Both were extremely loving toward one another and toward my sisters and me. They also instilled in me and my siblings a sense of commitment to community and an impatience with any sort of injustice: racism, sexism, or homophobia.

We were part of what I call "the invisible working class"— people who work multiple jobs to make sure there is food on the table, and to make sure their kids are educated. My stepdad didn't go to college. My mom attended college for one year. Yet they are both extremely intelligent. They exposed us early on to writers like Langston Hughes, Ralph Ellison, and James Baldwin.

My parents were deeply committed to our education. They enrolled me in an Afrocentric pre-K program called New Era Academy that served as a great foundation for my self-pride and self-confidence. As I got older, I attended Baltimore city schools, which are 90 percent black, and they moved us into neighborhoods that allowed us to attend the better schools, even if it meant we lived in smaller apartments. They advocated for us with our teachers. My twin sisters are freshmen in college now. When I think about the fruit of my parents' diligence and commitment, it's pretty great: they are likely to have three college graduates, despite their own limited educational opportunities.

My mother's advocacy was especially important when I was in elementary school and I experienced in a visceral way how pernicious subtle prejudice can be. I was a shy kid, didn't speak up much in class. I was so quiet, in fact, that my teacher didn't think I knew how to read. I got high grades on my papers and tests, and the teacher called my mom and accused me of cheating. The teacher thought I was copying other people's work. This made no sense to my mom, since I'd always read above my grade level. Her response was fierce. It began gently enough with "I've been reading to him since he was two years old. He can clearly read; he's just a shy kid." But that was only the beginning.

My mom then discovered that other students were being treated similarly: the teacher was assuming they couldn't do the work and accusing them of cheating. So she got organized. She brought together other parents whose kids were being given short shrift, and they brought to light this pattern of discriminatory behavior. As a result, my teacher was let go and replaced with another teacher, under whom we all thrived.

It was a lesson to me in the importance of standing up for what you believe in and also the power of network-building. Without my mom building a coalition of parents with the same issue, I might have been burdened with the label of cheater. It makes you consider how many other kids are being sabotaged by prejudiced teachers.

✦

When I was in high school I really came into my own as far as my language arts skills. I joined the debate team and became a skilled debater, surprising for someone who was so shy in elementary school. We'd travel to fancy prep schools, the kind that would cost a family $20,000 per year, and we'd win. I was gaining confidence in my intellect, in my power to communicate.

It was during this time that I wrote a paper for an English class and the teacher who handed it back to me said, "Rodney, you really should consider being a writer. You're a talented writer; I think that you could have a bright future in writing." I was floored and inspired. It was the first time anyone other than my parents had really endorsed me.

Writing and debate helped galvanize my path, allowed me to break out. I discovered that I had a voice and I had a gift: intellectual ability. I realized that I wanted to do things that would allow me to have a positive impact on the world by thinking, writing, talking about it, and connecting people.

In my first career, I was a freelance journalist in Baltimore. I wrote on issues of race, class, and politics for *Baltimore City Paper* and *Urbanite* magazine. I covered topics ranging from politics to education to transportation to arts and entertainment. One of my most memorable pieces was an essay following the election of President Barack Obama, describing a personal experience with the prejudiced white underclass and how my position as a newly minted black college graduate with middle class aspirations allowed me to ignore their prejudice—to acknowledge a new iteration of "black power" rooted in my own socioeconomic status relative to my white underclass neighbors at the time.

In my current career, I do advocacy with different stakeholder groups and I connect people and resources.

I am the regional leader for BMe in Baltimore. BMe celebrates black men as societal assets and works to help build caring and prosperous communities. We connect people of all genders and races to inspiring black men who create positive change and work in the areas people care about. We're an asset-rich network focused on people—all people—as assets we can build upon.

◆

My work with BMe has a different cast every day, which is part of the fun of it. On a basic level, I'm a community-builder, a networker, a resource connector. One day I'm working closely with BMe leaders who receive our grants, helping them strategize around program development or solve an issue they are facing. Another day I'm working to bridge opportunities between the local corporate and foundation communities back to the broader black community. On a third day, I'm at a policy forum, helping to shape a scaled approach to an issue affecting the city.

I want to be clear: I'm not an *expert* at anything. But I'm connected into so many different networks that I can make sure underrepresented voices are heard and that different constituencies can better understand one another. I help create win-win situations wherein resources flow to the black community and the talent that resides in the black community has an avenue to contribute positively to the growth of the city of Baltimore.

You'd be surprised at the number of times a corporate or foundation leader says, "Man, I wish I could be connected to some of the leaders in the community." My job is to ensure that they are, that the dialogues and collaborations are initiated for the broader benefit not just of the black community but of the city of Baltimore as a whole.

In addition to my work at BMe, I cofounded SocEnt Baltimore, a network of almost one thousand individuals who are social entrepreneurs, nonprofit innovators, and civic leaders in Baltimore. My cofounders are Pres Adams and Michelle Geiss. Our network aims to support these folks who strive to make our city better. The tie that binds is that we're all focused on social change and social justice. We host breakfasts at which emerging leaders speak, and we've created a coworking space called 34 East 25 where many organizations are housed and can collaborate and grow, including BMe.

◆

When one thinks about the fields of social entrepreneurship and innovation, it's easy to think of an industry dominated by white people. But what I'm really happy about is that in Baltimore, the face of social entrepreneurship and innovation actually happens to be me: a black male. It wasn't deliberate; it just happened. But I think it opens possibilities for everyone to think differently.

For example, when one sees a community activist who has been running a free meals program for twenty years, one doesn't immediately say, "That person is a social entrepreneur." But because I am one of the faces of social entrepreneurship here in Baltimore, I can help black people see the work they are doing in a new social entrepreneurial light—and I can help others in the community see it as well. I like that I'm part of an effort that crosses racial and class lines, an effort that fosters an empathic connection across different spheres.

All of this leads me to my main point: We've got to change the context and the conversation around black men. We have to change it away from a focus on black male survival, and start tapping into the creativity and the talents that exist among black males. We need to talk about how black males can help innovate solutions to issues in our community.

And it has to be about more than just empowering black men. It has to be about empowering their networks, their families, about plugging into people who are already operating effectively in the community but with limited resources. We will achieve justice and we will improve our communities when we can truly work together and become connected with empathy.

Rashid Shabazz

AGE: 40

TITLE: Vice President of Communications, Campaign for Black Male Achievement

COMMUNITY: Brooklyn, NY

Language is everything. One of the first things you do as a parent is read your child stories. The way we transmit values as a society is through storytelling.

When I was working as a grant seeker for nonprofits, I always felt uncomfortable because we would have to use "deficit language" to talk about any of the issues around young Black men and boys. It was like, "at-risk youth," "delinquent youth," "marginalized youth," "youth on the corner," "disconnected youth." That type of language didn't affirm the young people I was working with and how they saw themselves.

That's why when I came to work for the Open Society Foundation, I was so glad that the manager at my program, Shawn Dove, named his grant-making program the Campaign for Black Male Achievement. It was funny, when I first joined, people had quizzical looks on their faces when they heard the

name—a lot of people couldn't even fathom "Black male" and "achievement" being in the same line. It was almost like it was an oxymoron.

◆

I didn't start talking until I was four. A lot of my parents' friends assumed I was mute. I actually had a speech impediment. I was lucky that both my parents were supportive and took time off work to bring me to a speech pathologist. I always find it an interesting parallel that my life has been about journalism, communication, and trying to tell the stories of the Black community when, early on in my own life, I didn't even speak.

I lived in Bensonhurst, Brooklyn, in the Marlboro projects, until 1982, when I was seven. Marlboro was a diverse community with a mix of mostly Puerto Ricans, Jews, and Blacks, but the area surrounding the projects was an Italian community that did not take too kindly to others who weren't like them. I learned early the role race plays in everyday interactions.

My father and mother were in the Nation of Islam and stressed a strong sense of pride in their community and people. They were intent on affirming our cultural identity and self-worth. They always reinforced in our home the importance of knowledge of self, knowing who you are, respecting your history; knowing that Black people have been and are contributors to society and the world, and that you can be anything you want to be if you put your mind to it.

I grew up in a Black Nationalist home, but all my friends were very diverse. My parents always affirmed that if you're able to love yourself, you're better able to love your community and those around you, regardless of their ethnicity or race, which makes it easier to be a true humanitarian.

In 1983, when I was eight, we moved to Virginia. It was a

huge change. In Brooklyn, I had lived in this confined space where everyone knew each other. Sure, there was racial tension, but there was also a sense of community. The South was different. You were able to see the history of race relations in a much more immediate way. I remember on one trip to Wilson, North Carolina, I witnessed an actual Klan march. This was 1986. I watched it peeking out of my hotel window. It wasn't just history, it was still happening.

One time when I was twelve I was at the house of a friend who was white. His parents walked in the door, and they were talking to each other about some young Black men they had seen on the corner. His stepfather said to his mother, "These niggers on the corner need to get a life," or something like that. I was sitting right there. When he and his wife saw me, they tried to apologize. He said, "I hope you understand what I meant. You're not like them." It was almost like he was saying, "They're the niggers. You're not a nigger." But in my mind either we all were or we all weren't.

◆

In high school I started to become more politicized in my thinking.

I was a junior in high school in 1989, the year of the "Greekfest riots" out on Virginia Beach. Greekfest was this festival where a lot of young Black folks came down to the beach to party, and that year the police came out in their riot gear and just started swinging. It became a really big deal in Virginia and even nationally—Chuck D, the leader of the legendary rap group Public Enemy, memorialized it in "Welcome to the Terrordome."

The following year I was a senior class president of my high school. Even though I had grown up in a very political or socially conscious home, surrounded by Black institutions and seeing

my father going to work with Black men in jail, my thinking wasn't necessarily around activism. But as a Black senior class president, I started to see the structural racism that occurred. It was clear to me that I was being treated differently—I had a harder time raising funds than past presidents, and more of my decisions were called into question.

When I got to choosing a college, I was looking for a school with a sense of activism among the students. I went to James Madison University and joined the Black Student Alliance, started organizing on campus. Then one my friends from the BSA—Kirk Henny—introduced me to a book called *Black Men: Single, Obsolete, Dangerous?* by Haki Madhubuti.

I was nineteen at the time. I read the book over the summer, and it aligned with all the things I grew up seeing and knowing and experiencing. Madhubuti outlines a vision of what it takes for Black men to be healthy contributors to their community and the world. In many ways, the book is a blueprint for successful Black men. It made me realize I needed to be doing something more specific around telling the stories of the Black community, but more importantly I needed to be helping to build institutions that could tell our stories free of being over-editorialized or controlled.

I spent the summers of my junior and senior years in Chicago, interning at Madhubuti's publishing company, Third World Press. Seeing it was almost like seeing a dream in reality. He was so committed to sharing stories about Black Americans, building institutions, and connecting communities. It confirmed my belief that I wanted to do the same.

I ended up going to Yale for a master's in African studies, then Columbia Graduate School of Journalism. For a while I worked as a freelancer on political issues for a hip-hop magazine. I was merging all my favorite things—hip-hop, publishing, and writing about issues in the Black community. I was

helping change perceptions around Black Americans—or, more accurately, helping elevate the perceptions that are real and honest and true.

<p style="text-align:center">✦</p>

In my early twenties I was also introduced to the work of Marlon Riggs. Riggs had two powerful documentaries, one called *Ethnic Notions* and one called *Color Adjustment*. They really captured the full history of the caricatures and stereotypes of Blacks in this country.

If you look at the history of Black people in America, there's been almost five hundred years of policy, from the slave codes to the Black codes, driven by the idea that Black people are subhuman, that they're not fully human. In order to advance those polices, you first have to dehumanize an entire people. Because if they are human, and therefore equal to you, then you can't drive those policies, because you'd be putting yourself in that same paradigm.

I think a lot about how we can ensure that our humanity is fully at the forefront. Because we *are* human. But how do we ensure that we are telling accurate stories promoting accurate perceptions that will counter the dehumanizing aspect that has taken place?

I put a lot of those ideas into practice throughout my twenties and thirties working as a communications strategist at a series of nonprofit organizations—the Youth Development Research Fund, the Prison Moratorium Alliance, the Drug Police Alliance. My role was always to think about ways we could advance campaigns by telling the story of the people working on it and the people affected by the issue—how we could move the conversation forward.

In 2008, when I was working for Fenton Communications in New York, I attended a convening at the Ford Foundation.

This was right after Obama had been elected. The topic of the meeting was whether we could really change the cultural perceptions of Black men and boys. I thought the answer was yes, but I could see a lot of people around the table weren't convinced.

When I left that meeting, my colleague Robert Perez and I drafted a white paper called "Seize the Moment." I knew that we had to seize that moment to think about how President Obama's election changed things—what did it mean to be a Black male today?

In some ways, the white paper was my vision for the work I do now as a program officer for the Campaign for Black Male Achievement. At the time I could not have imagined we would see the creation of President Obama's My Brother's Keeper initiative to improve life outcomes for boys and men of color, but I also could not have imagined the death and murder of Trayvon Martin and the acquittal of George Zimmerman and the groundswell of movement and support that emerged. The convergence of all these events reinforced this notion of seizing the moment.

✦

If we use language like "disconnected," "marginalized," we won't be able to create a movement. We'll be creating individuals who feel further disconnected and unengaged—in all honesty, hopeless. But asset-based and affirming language gives you a sense of hope. Even when there's the reality of the challenge ahead, there is a sense that maybe we can win this. Maybe I can do something. Maybe I'm able to achieve.

At the Campaign for Black Male Achievement, we have funded projects around empowering Black men and boys to tell their own stories. For us, seizing the moment since 2008 has meant helping support networks and community-building

efforts to support our fathers, sons, brothers, uncles, and grandfathers. It is also a movement of women and girls and people who know that the challenges Black men and boys face also impact them.

We've worked within the entertainment industry, working with the powers that be to help change mainstream perceptions through movies and film and media. We've funded Color of Change, BMe, and other organizations to counter negative images of Black men and boys and promote positive images.

We've seen success. There was one reality TV show that was in production a couple years ago with the Oxygen Network about this rapper in Atlanta, Shawty Lo, called *All My Babies' Mamas*. Shawty Lo had had something like eleven or twelve kids with ten different women. And the show was going to be about the drama of that experience. Color of Change felt that that was reinforcing a negative stereotype, and they organized a campaign to make sure the show never came out—both online, mobilizing on social media, and offline, door-to-door. And the show never went on air.

When I began working at the Campaign for Black Male Achievement, I started a Google Alert for "Black males." When I started in 2009, I saw a lot of stories about "three Black males rob a liquor store," or stories about home invasion. But by near the end of 2011, it was different. You'd still have those same local news stories, but you'd also have stories about Obama. And I saw a major uptick in stories about Black males as assets, about Black male achievement. Recently you see stories about My Brother's Keeper. A lot of our grantees' stories have become mainstream. The groups that we're supporting are out there capturing a more diverse, accurate portrayal of Black men and boys.

To me, that's a shift that's not to be taken lightly.

Mel Mason

AGE: 72

TITLE: Psychotherapist; Cofounder, Executive Director, and Clinical Director, The Village Project, Inc.

COMMUNITY: Seaside, CA

I was born in a small coal-mining town called Providence, Kentucky, in 1943, at the height of Jim Crow segregation—white and colored fountains, a clear message that if you're black, you didn't stay downtown after dark.

My mother was an agent for one of the largest black-owned insurance companies. She often forwent her commission so that her customers could have the life insurance or burial insurance coverage they needed. My father was drafted into the army a few months after I was born, and he fought in World War II. He left for Europe when I was a tiny baby, and came back from the war suffering from what was then called "shell shock," now understood as post-traumatic stress disorder. For all of his life he struggled with alcohol and violence, and soon after his return, he left our home and was never a permanent fixture there again.

By middle school, my friends and I had begun fighting white boys who had been attacking us whenever we were uptown coming home from the segregated theater. My mother knew this was a recipe for winding up dead or in jail. When I was thirteen, she moved us to Seaside, California, to the promise of good jobs and a better life outside the strictures of the South.

In 1958, my mother married my stepfather, Walker Wells. He was a person I relied on for support from the time I was fifteen, even though I caused him difficulties in the early days. He was a strong man and one of my greatest role models. From him I learned what it was to be a man. From him, I learned about hard work, responsibility, and ethical bearing. He was a great father, and as a result, in later years, I would always qualify the title of "stepfather" when I talked about him to other people.

✦

Even with my mother and stepfather trying to hold me on the right course, I found a crowd in Seaside with whom I partied, drank, and did drugs. I became a functioning alcoholic. At one point my mother compared me directly to my father. I couldn't believe she saw me acting like a man that I claimed I hated.

It was at Monterey Union High School that I discovered my unique talent for basketball. After I graduated, I attended Monterey Peninsula College (MPC), where I had an incredible freshman year as a forward on the basketball team. To this day, I hold the all-school scoring and rebounding records at MPC, and I'm the only player in the school's history to be an All-American.

My coach at MPC, Larry Cummins, became like a family member to me. I'd first gotten to know Larry when he was an opposing coach whose team we beat while I was at Monterey

Union. He was a key figure, along with my mom and my stepdad, who supported me as I struggled with alcohol, drugs, and fighting. Yet despite my success, I dropped out of college after my freshman year, at age seventeen. It was a combination of immaturity, boredom, and a yearning for some kind of adventure.

I enlisted in the air force and was stationed overseas in Turkey and Germany. I figured I'd do a four-year tour and see the world. I developed a reputation as one of the best basketball players ever to don the uniform. But I also clashed with some of the Southern white noncommissioned officers who mistook my racial pride for insubordination. One of the white officers challenged me to a fight, which landed him on the ground and me in the stockade for six months.

I tried to hide the fact that I was incarcerated from my mother. However, my grandfather passed away during that time, and she contacted me through the Red Cross so I could come home to attend his funeral. I was locked up, so I wasn't able to travel. The pain in my mom's voice when we finally spoke, at the thought of her son behind bars, and the loss I felt at not being able to pay my last respects to my grandfather, were powerful. That almost killed me.

I wasn't ready to get reflective—I was angry. But I resolved to serve out my time in the military without incident. Unfortunately, my reputation for being a troublemaker was set, and upon my return stateside I was constantly provoked by officers who saw me as a target. I got in another fight and received a "Bad Conduct Discharge," which was later revised to "Honorable Discharge" with the help of a senator.

✦

I returned to Seaside and got right back into drinking, partying, and causing trouble. Then an important thing happened. In 1966, two friends of mine, guys I grew up with, were shot and

killed. They, like all of us, had made enemies. One was gunned down in front of a nightclub and the other one was shot while sitting in his car, when two guys, also black, ran up and shot him in the chest at least twice.

One night shortly after the death of these two young men a group of my friends met on the street corner where we would hang out, and we talked. Some of us decided that this was not the kind of life we had been raised to live. Others decided they were going to continue down the same path. Many of my friends in the latter group ended up dead or in prison. I decided to stop doing drugs and to go back to college. It would be years later, 1989, when I quit drinking alcohol.

Coach Cummins brought me back to MPC, where I finished my two-year associate's degree and set those scoring and rebounding records that still stand to this day. As my career at MPC wound down, I received scholarship offers from 104 colleges and universities. I was one of the top five junior college transfer recruits in the nation. I elected to go to Oregon State University, a fateful decision that would inform my racial consciousness even further.

◆

There were very few black people in Corvallis, Oregon, when I arrived to begin school. My first meeting with the coach, Paul Valenti, worried me, and it went downhill from there. The coach informed me that it would not be a good idea for me to walk around the campus at night. He forbade me from being in the town after dark.

For me, this smacked of the unwritten rules that governed Jim Crow–era Providence, Kentucky. I said, "I can go where I want." His response was "I'm letting you know the rules that you are going to have to abide by. If you do what I say, you'll be okay."

Shortly after that conversation, I went into town after dark. I was called into the coach's office the next day. He was yelling at me, swearing, and I was yelling and swearing right back. He stopped short of calling me uppity—he opted for "belligerent"—but I knew what he meant.

I saw the writing on the wall and realized that my days playing for this coach were limited. I began to study in a way that I had not before. I started talking to the other black athletes on campus about the inequities we faced. When the coach found out what I was doing, he withdrew my scholarship. I was gone before the season even started. I appealed to the NCAA with the help of Coach Cummins, but they ruled in favor of Oregon State. My playing days were done.

✦

After I left Oregon State, I moved back home to Seaside and later joined the Black Panther Party for Self-Defense. It was a revolutionary political party, started by Huey Newton and Bobby Seale back in '66, committed to liberating people from oppression.

I had moved to San Jose to work at Western Electric, and I was shocked at the racism I saw there. Along with some other workers I formed a group called Black Workers Unity to fight for better working conditions and equal opportunity. The company fired us, but that only brought on more protests, and they were forced to rehire us and concede to our demands. That is how I came to the attention of Bobby Seale and the Party.

It was one of the greatest learning experiences of my life. The Party gave me a framework within which to apply my race consciousness and my defiance, and it put the final touch on my trajectory: to not just help black people but to help oppressed people. I met people who inspired me and taught me—Huey Newton, Bobby Seale, Kathleen Cleaver, Masai Hewitt.

I received a real education in how capitalism creates class stratification. I learned to build coalitions with other organizations.

The Party offered a rare platform to mold an image of black males that wasn't about pimps or thugs or athletes and entertainers but rather about wholly self-possessed, intelligent leaders. It was about being a critical thinker—about being courageous in the face of power. If I had swallowed my pride at Oregon State, I may have gone to the NBA, but I would not have developed this social consciousness.

It was during this time that I became close to another towering mentor, Stephen E. Ross. Mr. Ross was one of the first blacks to be elected to any office in Central California. By 1978 he was mayor of Seaside, and he was a surrogate father figure to many young black males in the town. Mr. Ross expressed concern about some of my more radical political views, but he supported me nonetheless. After he was elected mayor, he made me chair of his Mayor's Advisory Committee over the objections of some of his peers. On the basis of that work, I ran for Seaside City Council and won a seat.

◆

In the years since, I've served in various roles in municipal politics. I've been inducted into the California Community College Athletic Association's Hall of Fame. I've served as president of the Monterey Bay Chapter of the NAACP, where I focused on challenging police brutality, discrimination in all forms, and achieving equal pay for equal work. I've run campaigns to become governor of California and president of the United States.

But today, my biggest impact comes from the community-building work I do with blacks, particularly black males, through The Village Project, Inc. Our mission is to help the community, particularly the African-American community,

reach a greater state of well-being through the delivery of community-based, culturally specific, and culturally competent services.

I was inspired to get into counseling because of my time in the Black Panther Party and the social work we did in the black community. I started professional counseling in the early seventies, becoming a therapist in 1990—I am still the only licensed black male therapist in Central California. My clinical approach is informed as much by my personal experience as it is by more traditional things like my training and case experience. So both of my projects try to ground personal progress in strategies and methodologies that respect black culture.

One of our key initiatives at The Village Project is a young men's group called Handling the Pressures of Life. It was started by a man named Ted Black, a Seaside native who spent time in prison as a young adult. Once a week, Ted meets with a group of at-risk young black males. He takes them through a curriculum he developed, focused on building self-esteem, managing stress, and identifying and leveraging one's strengths in order to be a good father, brother, teacher. The young men in the program also attend city council meetings and volunteer with school age kids and at homeless shelters—they cultivate themselves while contributing to their community. Ted's efforts have led to many kids graduating from high school, attending college, gaining professional skills, and building stable lives, and The Village Project has continued to grow.

This work is done in tandem with my clinical practice at the Black Family Resource Center. In my own experience, so much of building self-esteem and channeling one's energy productively is about knowing your history and your community's history and then working through that history, working through that cultural heritage. This is the approach that I take in working with the people I counsel. It's also the approach that

I teach to young people of color who are training to become social workers and therapists.

I'm pretty certain that I could have made it to the NBA if my time at Oregon State had played out differently. Still, it turned out to be a blessing. I've lived a long life, and I've been blessed to spend most of it countering the effects of racism and discrimination through education, activism, and counseling. I eventually made peace with my dad, a few years before he passed away. Through family support, mentorship from coaches and family friends, and passions for basketball and social change-making, I ended up all right.

Justin Davis

AGE: 33

TITLE: Program Officer/Impact Advisor,
College Bound Brotherhood

COMMUNITY: Oakland, CA

My first role model lived in the room next to me. He was my brother, thirteen years my senior, and a high school baseball and basketball star. As soon as I could walk, I was slipping into his jerseys and sitting in my mother's lap watching his games, emulating the spins, catches, and shots I saw him make. My brother's room was covered by posters of eighties sports royalty—Edwin Moses, a young Michael Jordan, and George "Iceman" Gervin. Too scared to ever fully enter, I would peek through the doorway imagining myself on one of those larger-than-life posters.

After seeing my favorite player, Magic Johnson, win back-to-back championships, I knew exactly what it was that I wanted to be—a professional basketball player. Although I didn't consider being an entertainer or athlete the only measure

of black success, like many inner city youth I considered that path to be much more realistic than becoming the next Cliff Huxtable.

I grew up in a middle class family in Berkeley, California. My dad was a hardworking blue-collar man and high school dropout from Chicago. My mom was a middle school teacher who began every summer worrying about being reassigned or laid off. While Pete showed me what a day's hard work looked and felt like, Betty nurtured and cultivated my curiosity in education, arts and culture, and life.

When I reached high school, my hunger to excel academically led to an isolation that was full of irony. Although the school was at least 50 percent black or Latino, most periods I walked into a classroom where I was the only black male in the class. That environment became challenging to thrive in socially. I noticed that my classmates would pick me first to be on their team in PE, but in the classroom they were not thrilled to work with me. I believed that my white and Asian peers perceived my athleticism as an ancestral endowment and my presence in the classroom as a result of tokenism rather than meritocracy. It angered me and drove me to be as competitive in the classroom as I was on the court.

As I began to spend more time before, during, and after school studying wherever I could find a sturdy surface, my black friends started calling me whitewashed and engaged me differently. They'd say, "Oh, you're trying to be uppity. I see you in all these high-level classes. Who do you think you are?" To dismiss their accusations, I often elbowed my way to become the center of foolishness, telling them, "Nah, I'm still down." I eventually perfected this dance between these juxtaposed worlds.

✦

The reconciliation I would need to move forward came while I was on the basketball court. The court served as a sanctuary; a place where I could just be me. I didn't need to continuously prove that I was as intelligent as my peers or cool enough to say what's up to my boys in the hallways. As my skills developed and were tested on the Amateur Athletic Union traveling circuit (circus would be apropos), I got to play against the top talent in the country.

Even though few of us were predicted to go pro straight from high school, I would fantasize about the idea. My family quickly brought me Back down to earth. They reminded me that although my goal was to get to the NBA, I'd get there through college. I still remember my mother pulling me aside and saying, "Justin, don't forget about your academics. Put your academics first. Basketball will be your platform, but your academics will carry you through life."

My mother often referenced my brother's experience as an example. My brother had passed on a scholarship opportunity to go to Santa Clara University, a midlevel Division I institution known for its strong academics, in hopes of playing big-time college basketball at Georgetown University. He opted for a community college, hoping it would bridge him to Georgetown. That never happened, and it took him more than thirteen years to receive his undergraduate degree.

In the end, there were several college options on the table in terms of an elite basketball experience that would prepare me for the next level. However, once the process came to an end, I felt Stanford University was the only school that demonstrated a bigger picture—acquiring the tools needed to succeed and then thinking innovatively about how best to use them.

✦

Stanford was the challenge that I expected it to be. But the experiences of being perceived as too tall, too athletic, and too dark to be intellectually capable helped me quickly adjust to the lack of diversity on campus and the academic rigor.

Basketball proved to be challenging at times as well. During my junior and senior year, at Stanford I sustained the same injury—a slight tear of the medial collateral ligament. There's never a good time for an injury, but at that critical point, when I needed to prove myself to NBA scouts, it was disheartening. The majority of the hurt I felt was not from the injury itself, but from realizing that my dream of playing in the NBA was slipping away.

I entered Stanford with the goal of playing professional basketball, and before my injuries, anything short of that would have been a failure to me. But as I was recovering, my family reminded me why I was in college in the first place: to obtain a degree. So rather than dwell on what might or might not happen with basketball, I channeled that energy toward completing my degree. I began taking classes in education. Teaching was something I could see myself doing not only if professional basketball didn't work out, but even if it did.

As it happened, I recovered from my injuries and I was ultimately offered a contract to play professional basketball. Within two months of receiving my degree in communications, I was on a flight to Greece to play First Division basketball, the most competitive level in Europe.

Now, instead of being the only African-American in the classroom, I was seemingly the only African-American in the whole city of Patras. No longer concerned with racial landscapes, I was able to focus on my purpose: becoming a professional and developing my craft.

I worked hard in Patras and was eventually offered a contract with the Golden State Warriors, my hometown NBA team. It

was a short but memorable experience. Even though my time with the team only lasted for one month, I could honestly tell myself, "Justin, through hard work you've reached your dream as a twenty-three-year-old." It validated that anything is possible through hard work and commitment.

I would later find myself continuing my career back in Europe, eventually facing even more severe injuries than I had while in college. They say that through age comes wisdom. This time around, I was better able to weather the storm of physical pain and mental hurdles. I took a critical look at my prospects and did a cost-benefit analysis. For years I had sacrificed my body and health to play a game that I loved and that had provided me so much—an elite education, cultural exposure, and a resilience to persevere through adversity. I made the conscious decision to pursue a career outside of basketball.

✦

At the age of twenty-eight, I moved back to Berkeley, California, to the home I grew up in. Pivoting from basketball was an adjustment. I had a degree, but didn't necessarily know what to do with it. That left me feeling empty and lost.

While on long walks with my dog, perhaps subconsciously searching for answers, I became reacquainted with the community that raised me. I saw what had changed and a lot of what hadn't. I'd walk through Grove Street Park, where I had played ball as a kid, and notice how there was always a presence of youth throughout the school day. I would think to myself, shouldn't these guys be in school or just doing something a little more productive than "just chillin'"? Being the person that I am, I began engaging them, curious to hear what their story was and what they were seeking.

Implicitly or explicitly, anyone could consider these young men as threatening. But if you were to have meaningful conver-

sations with them, you would quickly realize that they were just as bright, loving, and caring as anyone else. In hanging at the park, these brothers offered each other love, support, comfort, and protection. In fact, most of them had felt abandoned by the educational system and tightly held on to the grudges they had with former teachers. So rather than defend themselves against write-ups and in-house suspensions, they relegated themselves to the park, a place where they could be themselves.

It would not be long after that first walk through Grove Street Park that I would land upon what my purpose was postbasketball—working directly with young men and helping them prepare for college and beyond. Some of their experiences reminded me of ones that I had in which I felt "less than."

I soon pursued opportunities that could put me directly in front of black males and allow me to use my experiences as a template for helping them understand the value of a college education. After nearly two years of being at home I found a job in the College Bound Brotherhood, a program of the Mitchell Kapor Foundation. The Brotherhood was led by its brainchild, Cedric Brown, and it focused on supporting community-based organizations that nurtured college access and readiness for high-school-age black males. As fate would have it, Cedric saw me as an ideal individual to lead his initiative and aid him in moving the agenda forward.

✦

It's been four years since I teamed up with Cedric. Together, we have deepened our reach and have encouraged these young men to be unapologetic about having a "college is for me" attitude. However, we know that college readiness is only a piece, albeit a significant piece, of the solution. In this age of digital inundation, we look to inform youth on how tech skills are

necessary for competing in the twenty-first-century workforce and economy.

As it stands today, young black men have far less access to opportunity around tech innovation than their white and Asian peers. That gap has created a pipeline issue in the tech industry. Right now, a dismal percentage of black professionals work in the tech industry. The irony is that a significant number of young black males grow up in challenging environments that force them to be innovators and creators. Moreover, the black community is one of the largest consumers of tech (including social media apps). But we aren't the proprietors.

If we can marry this proclivity for innovation with the technical skills to create new products, then something special will undoubtedly crystalize. Being tech savvy can be just as much a part of our own expectations and dreams as being an athlete or entertainer.

It is time we change the narrative. It's time for a shift in mind-set.

As I reflect, I see that shifting careers has been humbling and greatly rewarding. It exposed me to a path far more rewarding and impactful. It has given me an opportunity to give back to my community, a community that I've always been a part of, a community that has given me so much, and one to which I will always remain connected, whether it be through work or a casual walk through the park.

✦

This is my responsibility as a black man: to support, develop, and nurture the greatness of the young black men who will come after me. That's what makes me happy; and seeing young black men striving toward greatness makes me even happier.

My dad always told me to find myself a job that didn't feel like work. Basketball never felt like work. That's why I loved it.

It made me most happy in life. But working with these young brothers and seeing their appreciation for having someone who cares, who wants to make their lives better, who calls them by their names, who listens to what they have to say—that puts everything in its proper perspective and definitely doesn't feel like work.

Horace Madison

AGE: 49

TITLE: Business and Financial Manager

COMMUNITY: Harlem, NY

My dad was killed when I was seven. He was shot in a bar in Harlem. He loved the streets, everybody loved him. He had gone from being a Golden Gloves boxer to being a street enforcer. Later he'd gotten a real job and became a manager at a construction site. My mom, shall we say, "helped" him along that path to a real job, assisting him with getting his GED.

After his death, my mom was on a mission to get me out of Harlem as soon as she could. I sort of negotiated a deal with her that if I agreed to leave Harlem, she would allow me to attend public school. I'd been attending one of the best private schools in Manhattan, Columbia Grammar. I was there from first through sixth grade. After school I'd leave the predominantly white confines of Columbia Grammar, to take public transportation to my home in Harlem. Back then Harlem was predominantly, if not entirely, Black and Latino. Not the really

nice, comfortable, diverse Harlem of today. There was this enormous dichotomy between those two worlds.

I remember at school we would have career day, and these private school kids were claiming they wanted to be a CEO, CFO, COO, etc.

I asked my mom about these letters that the kids were throwing out at school. I was ready to make up some letters of my own, you know. My mother said, "You know those people we see on the subway with the suits and the briefcases? You know those big buildings in midtown? That's where they work. Those are some of the richest, most powerful people in the world."

Right then and there, I told myself that's what I wanted to be.

But then after school I would come back home, back uptown, and I realized that the other kids in my neighborhood had very different aspirations. You had kids talking about, at best, wanting to be a fireman, and at worst, wanting to run numbers, or wanting to be a pimp. So I went back to my mother and asked her about that—"How come everybody around here—my boys Chris, Ivan, Tony—how come they don't aspire for the same things I do?"

She said, "How can you aspire for something when you don't even know it exists?"

That put things in perspective. So I told my mom, okay, I want to wear a suit and have a briefcase and be one of those rich guys in the high-rise in midtown. But I want to do it so I can expose our people to those things, educate our people, Black and Latino people, so they can want this too. I was ten years old.

✦

In sixth grade I moved up to White Plains in Westchester County, the suburbs of New York City. The burbs were where people from Harlem and the Bronx aspired to go—it was defi-

nitely an upgrade. But for my mom, it was more than that. It was aspirational, but it was also about protecting me.

When we moved, part of the agreement I made with my mom was that I wouldn't have to go to private school anymore. I could now go to public school. I found that public school in the burbs was way more diverse than private school in the city. I played quarterback on the football team. My tailbacks and receivers were Black, my fullback was Italian white, and my center was German white. I also played basketball, where the team was mostly black. I was on the baseball team too; that team was mostly white and with a couple of Hispanics. So I learned to be comfortable with a lot of different types of people. I knew I could exist with white people. I certainly knew I could exist with Black and Latino people.

It also helped that I was a really good athlete, in three sports. I was confident. And it didn't hurt that I came from Harlem, so I had that Harlem swag.

◆

I learned about the importance of financial literacy early on.

My grandfather was a professional drummer, and he would tell me about all these musicians and the notorious stories about how they would get taken advantage of. They just didn't understand what they were working with. They didn't understand the business of music publishing. My dad, having been a Golden Gloves boxer, would tell me all these stories about boxers who didn't know anything about handling money and would get taken advantage of. Then of course I would hear about Mike Tyson going bankrupt, and even before that, Joe Louis working in a parking lot in Las Vegas. It was sad. But, little did I know at the time, the stories from my grandfather and my father would be the inspiration behind my career helping people with financial literacy.

Financial literacy is really just having some basic under-standing about money—banking, borrowing, lending, interest rates, etc. Blacks and Latinos generally do not have the same access to early education or resources, which means we don't have the same understanding of these vehicles and how they work. In the end, the systems end up intimidating us.

So I had constant reminders, reinforcements, about the ills that existed: the lack of financial awareness and the need for it. I didn't know it at the time, but all of this would lead me to my mission now, which is "empowering people" with financial literacy.

✦

I didn't start out trying to be "financial manager to the stars." I wanted to work as a financial guide to minorities—to bridge those two worlds I had experienced in my childhood. It just so happened that those minorities would turn out to be stars.

When I first started as a financial planner I was working with teachers. Then one day I saw a girl in the subway singing a song. Her name was Patti Rothberg. My good friend Alicia and I saw the talent in her. We created a bidding war between two major labels, by thinking outside the box. That ultimately led to a million dollars, between her recording and publishing deals. In the process of finding Patti a business manager, I met the business manager for Puff, Sean "Puffy" Combs, who still wasn't big yet. So I ended up working on Puff's account.

From there, I picked up three of the four producers Puff called "the Hitmen." Those were the guys that were produc-ing all the tracks for Bad Boy Records, right when Bad Boy exploded. Via those producers I picked up Ma$e, Kelly Price, Carl Thomas, the Lox, and other clients from Bad Boy, and it just grew from there.

Over the course of time I've had some great clients, like

Outkast, Usher, DMX, Eve, Tyrese, Lil Jon, Lil Wayne, and others. I've had some good sports clients as well—Arian Foster, Glen "Big Baby" Davis, Stromile Swift.

My job is to help my clients prepare for the future because I know that most artists are not going to be hot forever. Sooner or later the stream of revenue slows down, and eventually it stops. Many entertainers think they can extend their career into other areas like Will Smith did. They're like, "Hey, I'm finished rapping, and now I'm going to go make movies for ten million dollars." It's just that that kind of thing happens so seldom.

These days I find that there are many musicians who aspire to be more than just musicians. They want to start businesses and build their empire, but they don't really know how. They want to be like Jay Z or like Puff, or like Dr. Dre, but the reality is that it's very difficult. If you don't understand inventory, you can't have a clothing line—at least not a successful one. If you don't understand gross versus net, you can't have a successful business of any type. You also need to have a really strong team around you—not just a business manager but also a personal manager, definitely at least one lawyer.

To help my clients make smarter decisions with their money, one of the tactics I've employed has sort of taken on a life of its own. Internally it was initially called "The Stupid Letter." When a client wanted to make a questionable purchase, I would fax over a letter and make the client sign it, acknowledging the fact that the decision was against my advice. The letter basically said that, just so we're clear, despite your initial desire and commitment to me to make good financial decisions and accumulate wealth and take care of your family and yourself, you have now decided that it is imperative that you "must" have a $50,000 watch.

Just to be clear, I wasn't telling the client that he or she was

stupid; I was documenting the fact that something the client was doing, some transaction that he or she wanted to embark upon, was a stupid transaction financially. Anyway, word got out, and it became so infamous that I would have clients tell me flat out, "Don't send me a stupid letter, 'cause I'm not signing it."

✦

More and more, I feel that there's a greater understanding that financial literacy is necessary, particularly with people of color.

Whether you're talking about the average everyday teenager, or whether you're talking about an athlete, entertainer, or celebrity, most do not maintain a high level of income over a lifetime. I think my celebrity clients are becoming more cognizant of the need to set themselves up to have a business or to do something after their performing or playing years. And all of that requires some form of financial literacy. You can't go into another business after you're done being a performer if you don't understand how business works.

I was talking to someone recently who said that sticking through the tough times is what gets you to the good times. I told her that I would take that a step further. I would say that the ability to weather the storm is what determines who really can and will be successful for the long run.

Anybody can be okay for a short period of time. As John Chaney, the great former Temple coach, said, "Let's not have any high-fiving and slapping asses." He didn't want players so drunk from emotion that they lost focus on the endgame—winning. Similarly, when managing your money, and your career even, you have to stay focused and make smart long-term decisions.

Many times artists, athletes, and entertainers don't realize how fortunate they are to have been successful in their trade.

Rarely do they have the know-how to convert their success into revenue streams that will last them over a lifetime. These celebrities have the ability to influence so many and to affect so many financially. And that's where I come in—I help them, so they, in turn, will influence others. That's financial literacy.

John Hope Bryant

AGE: 49

TITLE: Founder, Chairman, and CEO, Operation HOPE

COMMUNITY: Compton, CA; Atlanta, GA

I f the twentieth century was about erasing the color line, the twenty-first century will be about tackling class and poverty issues.

If you want to solve poverty, if you want to solve poor housing conditions, if you want to solve single-parent households, you need to focus on economics. I'm convinced that if black men today had the ability to produce gainful employment and wealth, if they had the respectability of ownership and opportunity, if they knew how to master this thing called free enterprise and take care of their families—I'm convinced they'd stay home, as fathers, husbands, and household leaders. You would not have 70 percent of black households run by women.

✦

I grew up in South Central LA, in Compton. My mother and my father were my first visible role models in life. I had the benefit of having a mom and a dad at home, which today, in the black community, seems as foreign as living on Mars.

My mother was a confident woman. She had a vision for herself. She passed those traits down to me. She told me she loved me every day of my life. And there's nothing more powerful than a child being told he or she is loved. It was her empowering me that provided me an understanding of the true nature of poverty.

I define wealth and poverty differently than most people. Part of what makes you poor is low self-esteem. It's a different from simply being broke. Broke is about economics. Poor embodies a disabling frame of mind, a depressive issue with your spirit. Being poor allows others to convince you that they know who you are, that they should make decisions on your behalf.

My parents owned a number of businesses. We had a gas station, an eight-unit apartment building, a cement contracting business, and a nursery. My mother ran the nursery because she wanted to spend more time with me, so she decided to let other people finance her time with her child, charging families fifteen bucks a week to take care of one kid and twenty-five bucks a week to take care of two. I was her first client, and if she could've charged me, she would have.

Luckily for me I didn't really understand what was going on underneath the visual message, which was a lot of drama. My mother was financially literate, but my dad controlled the money. My parents would argue over money because my dad didn't understand it—and he was too proud to admit he wasn't as knowledgeable as my mother. By my ninth birthday, my parents had divorced. We lost the apartment building, the gas station, the nursery, even our home. I moved with my mother

to Compton. It was after the divorce that she controlled her own destiny again. She also regained personal financial wealth.

✦

When I was nine, a man came to my classroom in Compton and started teaching financial literacy in a home economics class. I wasn't really interested in what he had to say. But I was interested in what he was wearing, and how he carried himself. He was wearing a blue suit, red tie, white shirt. He was a white guy, but the only color I could see was green. He said he was a banker that financed entrepreneurs. I didn't know what an entrepreneur was, but all of a sudden I wanted to be one.

✦

This man unpacked for me the language of money—what I call "the memo." It's a memo that too many black and brown people never get. The memo is about how free enterprise and capitalism work. It's about what the hell the *Wall Street Journal* is saying, what they're rambling about on Bloomberg TV. It's about what the local corner store means for the global economy, and how our tax money pays for everything from roads to gutters to the police officers.

All of this gave me a new respect and admiration for my dad. I saw how he was able to start his own businesses, and I wanted to be like him that way. So I started wearing suits to school. My mom made me the ugliest little velvet suits you can imagine. I was nine years old. I would get my ass whopped every day, but I realized early on that eagles don't fly in packs.

Soon enough I started selling things. I would buy mail order shoes and mail order jewelry, and sell it to my teachers at school. Every inner city kid's a great salesman.

If the banker was my first accidental mentor, my second

accidental mentor was Mr. Mack. Mr. Mack owned Mack's liquor store, down the street from my house in Compton. He sold liquor for adults and candy for kids—it was a horrible combination. I approached Mr. Mack one day and told him that he was selling the wrong kind of candy. He told me, "Go away, little boy. I have a college degree." I told him, "That's nice, but I have cavities, and I know what kind of candy kids want."

I kept bugging Mr. Mack, and finally he offered me a job. He said I could work at the counter, but I told him I wanted to be a box boy. He laughed, but gave me the job. I spent the next few weeks packing and unpacking boxes, and doing market research. I wanted to find out where he bought the doggone candy.

Once I confirmed that he was buying the wrong product, I quit and went into the candy business myself. With a loan from my mother, I went to Ira's Food Store and bought forty dollars' worth of candy. I ate half the inventory myself, but with the remaining twenty dollars' worth of candy, I was able to earn three hundred dollars by the end of the week.

Every light in my brain flipped on. I didn't have to ask my parents for money anymore. Also, I had never liked the idea that the liquor store was selling candy to kids; it felt wrong to me. But using my business sense, I put Mr. Mack out of the candy business.

I realized that if I could turn that switch for other people in my neighborhood, I could make a big difference.

✦

All of my old friends from my neighborhood are either still there or dead. Most of the ones who are alive are in prison, on probation, or on parole.

I think about my best friend, George. George was a bright

kid—while I was getting Cs, he was getting As. But George didn't have a daddy at home. His daddy had bounced, and he probably bounced because his own daddy had bounced years earlier. George's mother was doing the best she could by herself.

George didn't have anybody positive to model after. I had my dad—he wasn't living with us, but he was in touch. George had my next-door neighbor Tweet. And Tweet was a local gangster.

Tweet looked tough. He looked quick. He looked like he was in charge. This is what our neighborhoods do: we wing it with class; we wing it with style. We look at someone like Tweet and we say, because he looks good and because he's got money in his pocket and he's driving a nice car and he walks with a swagger, because the girls like him, that must be what success looks like. So we say, let me go be like him, because I sure don't see success anywhere else.

This is not dumb or stupid behavior. This is brilliant. We're modeling what we see. When what we see are rap stars, athletes, and drug dealers, how could we expect our kids to model anything else?

So right around the time that I started dressing like a businessman, George started dressing like Tweet, hanging out like Tweet, talking like Tweet. And when I was ten years old, making three hundred bucks a week selling candy, George got shot and killed on the corner with Tweet.

✦

So much of the intellectual firepower in the black community today is about fighting oppression. We have an entire industry of lawyers, civil rights organizations, institutes, think tanks, organizations focused around fighting oppression because we have a history of being oppressed. But fighting oppression is different than building an empowered community.

We have enough civil rights lawyers. If you are a young black person coming up today and you've been modeling good behavior, you've got the tools, and you're trying to make a difference in your community—you look around for symbols of success, and you see a lot of people like me and women fighting oppression. And that's very respectable and very understandable. But the model has changed from fifty years ago.

Back then it was necessary for all our young black men and women to become lawyers, to go into court and fight against injustice, to create a level playing field. Today, that's still important, but the issue of the day is economics.

We need Al Sharpton. We need the NAACP and the Urban League. But as much as we need defense attorneys, we also need business attorneys. We need our kids to be getting their degree in business and economics. We need them to become entrepreneurs, and to create some jobs.

It's a completely different solution that requires a completely different set of skills and tools. We need folks who can create a tax base in our neighborhoods and move credit scores and create homeowners and small-business owners and wealth. We need a whole new set of guys and girls who can create jobs because, to quote Van Jones, nothing stops a bullet like a job.

✦

The reason I have hope is that it's not like black and brown people got the memo and then screwed it up. We never got the memo. We haven't had the role models to teach us about what the *Wall Street Journal* is talking about, and how you can make a living wage, and why selling drugs and being willing to die protecting a corner that you don't even own is a bad business model.

That's the role modeling that I want to provide to our community going forward. I want people to say, "I heard about this

entrepreneur named John Hope Bryant, and I want to be like him." Or I want them to say, "I want to put John Hope Bryant out of business. I want to be his competitor, because I can do it ten times better than him."

But either way, I want them to say, "John Hope Bryant gave me the memo."

Trabian Shorters

AGE: 47

TITLE: CEO, BMe Community

COMMUNITY: Miami, FL

Millennials are the largest, most diverse, most digitally connected generation in American history. They will drive unprecedented changes in this country's future. If you count their role in electing the nation's first black president—twice—they already are. They are coming of age at the exact same time that the baby boomers—who have defined American priorities and personality for the last fifty years—are aging out. This tectonic shift in American identity is unstoppable. But what type of country we will have depends entirely upon the answer to the question "Who do you think you are?"

Knowing that tells you what you'll believe in, where you will belong, and how you will behave, because we all try to be who we think we are. The stories we tell each other create the lives we live.

✦

My story is one of matriculating through identities of poor black boy, genius nerd kid, national service leader, civil rights worker, successful tech entrepreneur, social investor, philanthropist, and now network builder. But in every phase I have remained, first and foremost, my grandfather's grandson.

Kennis Hutchons Sr., my grandfather, was a small, simple man from Texas who moved to Michigan at the end of World War II. He had four daughters and a son. He and my grandmother loved God, were married for sixty-five years, and died forty days apart, one in December 2009 and the other in January 2010. My mom was their third daughter and was only sixteen when I was born in 1967. I practically grew up in their home.

In 1972 my grandfather changed my life by introducing me to the "Love Doctrine." I was five years old, watching Jerry Falwell preach a terrifying sermon on TV about how we will be "cast down into the fiery furnace of hell for all time for our wicked deeds and thoughts." "For my thoughts!" I thought. "I'm doomed! I mean, I can probably control my actions pretty good, but my thoughts of cookies and Kool-Aid happen before I can stop them."

In a panic for my immortal soul, I ran to my grandfather and asked him, "Is it true that God will cast me down into the fiery furnace forever?" And my grandfather looked at me in that calm, loving way that he would for decades to come, and he introduced me to the Love Doctrine with these simple words: "God commands us to love one another the way that Jesus loves us. That's all you have to do."

I sighed the most relieved five-year-old sigh in the history of the world. "Okay. I can do that."

My grandfather was a Love Doctrine evangelist, which means he didn't preach love, he demonstrated it. For instance, when he retired from working in the factory, he started the New Life Christian Outreach Church. Many of his first members were guys fresh out of prison, so he started a job-placement service for them. Then he realized they often had no transportation, so he started a shuttle service to take them from home to work and back. When he saw that people needed food, he started a food pantry. When he saw that housing was an issue, the church started buying and refurbishing houses. The thing is, Grandpa did all this "loving" matter-of-factly, without grants or fanfare or even an eighth-grade education. It's men like him who make men like me. I realized later in life that black men like him are plentiful but forgotten in the stories we tell about who we think we are.

✦

My generation was the first one born into an "integrated America," but by 1982, when President Reagan declared the "War on Drugs," black males had gone from being portrayed as the faces of a movement for equality and justice to being the poster boys for America's fears. Crack cocaine was the catalyst. In the wake of a stalled economy it flooded neighborhoods like some sci-fi zombie virus, and the general public was terrorized by news accounts of drug-gang violence, inner-city decay, and the emergence of a "permanent underclass" created by generations of poverty and social isolation.

The barrage was so constant that by 1989, dramatic and horrifying stories of packs of black boys running amok in Central Park, raping middle-class white women for fun, and "raspy-voiced" black men shooting middle-class couples in Boston for no reason seized the American consciousness. Princeton political science professor John Dilulio coined the term "super-predator"

and described such inner city boys as "fatherless, Godless, and jobless." The horrifying tales above turned out to be totally untrue, but by then the image of the black male predator was firmly embedded in the minds of boomers and their children.

✦

Nobel Prize–winning research psychologist Daniel Kahneman would later point out in an unrelated study that the brain is prone to cognitive illusions, one of which is believing that "what you see is all there is." After the War on Drugs was declared, the unrelenting media campaigns showing black men as threats without a balanced portrayal of them as assets had a deeply perverting effect on America. What resulted were zero-tolerance laws, mandatory sentencing, and militarized police forces that assume that black boys are menaces to society who must be tracked and confronted, captured, or gunned down. It is a horrible and unfair way to view people, but I don't blame people for thinking that what they see is all there is.

Like many black people, I also picked up the habit of defining myself and other black males by our costs rather than our contributions. In 1991, a woman from Detroit named Octavia Wilson broke me of that blinding habit of explaining myself through the lens of a false perspective on black males. I was at a national conference on community service, and about a dozen black people who had met at the conference gathered to get to know each other better. The first brother, who was my age, introduced himself by saying "My name is so-and-so, I'm from thus-and-such. My dad wasn't in the home, my neighborhood was dangerous, and we had no positive black male role models, so that's why I now do what I do." Then I said, "My name is Trabian, and I'm from Pontiac, Michigan. My dad wasn't in the home, my neighborhood was dangerous, and we had no positive black male role models, so that's why I now do what I do."

The next guy started repeating the same refrain when Octavia, who was twice our age, interrupted with a pained expression on her face. "Why do you keep saying that?" she asked. "You mean to tell me that you never had an uncle or a grandfather, or your mom never dated a man who knew right from wrong? You really had *no* positive black male role models when you were growing up?"

It was as if she turned on a light in the room. I had all three of those types of men in my life, and by my lip-syncing the lie that "there are no positive black male role models," I had discounted the very men who made all the difference in my life. My grandfather was a minister; my uncle Charles was a former marine and current family man; and my mother dated a good man for many years who had a past as a gangster. The minister, the soldier, and the gangster role-modeled commitment to love, freedom, and family in ways that remain with me to this day. So I never again told the lie about there being no positive black male role models. And I began searching for a way for America to climb out of those hostile, denigrating narratives.

The next milestone happened on Monday, October 16, 1995. I attended the Million Man March and saw one million black men unmediated for the first time in my life. We were beautiful! We spent the entire day standing on the Mall in Washington, DC, hearing from generations of black leaders including Rosa Parks, who was greeted with men calling out her name in waves of sound that rolled from the back of the crowd to the front—soothing, exhilarating, and beautiful all at once.

The heads of the NAACP, the National Urban League, and dozens of other civil rights organizations and black church denominations refused to collaborate on or endorse the march because it was organized by Louis Farrakhan, but their members and congregants were there in droves. Three things stuck with me from this historic gathering:

1. Black men are loving men who want meaningful roles as the builders God made us to be.

2. The more than 837,000 of us who were there (according to ABC-TV-funded researchers at Boston University) will never forget the unmitigated dignity we felt. I remember us even picking up litter as we left the Mall. Black men held the most orderly, peaceful gathering that place has ever seen.

3. The apocalypse that America fears from black men isn't coming—quite the opposite. Black men are actually serving their country, starting businesses, and giving to charity more often than all other men in America, according to data from the army, the Census Bureau, and the *Cultures of Giving* report.

I also noticed that the oft-repeated refrain that black men are an "endangered species" fell out of usage immediately after the march. And the Million Man March punctuated something that Coretta Scott King had told me back in 1992: "They can deal with physical force, but there is no defense against soul force." Soul force is dignity—a word that literally means "being worthy of respect." It is self-love coupled with love of others. Martin Luther King Jr. once described this type of love as "Love standing against all that would oppose love."

◆

Looking back over my life, I understand that weird combination of arrogance and fear that I've seen behind the eyes of so many black men today. The popular narrative of black males as absent, as being problems or threats is enervating. That deep and wide societal ambience of unwantedness and invalidation

forces black boys and men to fight for their souls early and often.

I've seen many adjust to this denial of their virtue by becoming "better than black" business guys. I'm probusiness, but this type of businessperson lacks inner confidence, so his approach to business is often a denial of himself and his people. I've seen others become "extra black" hip-hop guys who respond to societal rejection with defiance and style that makes being undesirable look cool. Me, I became a lover of black people who affirms their virtues in every light.

But currently we all function amid a well-worn conclusion that we suck—that society doesn't need us, and, more important, that it doesn't want us. So we black males often feel that we must force ourselves on the world, as much with courage as with fear. We push forward with gaping holes in our game, which is a problem, because our women and our children need us to feel confident in our own skin—to love them and our people openly, without apology, and to love the rest of humanity because of it. It has become my life's mission to invest in people's better natures and to build more caring and prosperous communities inspired by black men and in cooperation with all members of the human family.

◆

When I came to the Knight Foundation in December 2007 as vice president of communities, I was asked to help shape transformative change in twenty-six cities and towns. When I left in July 2013 to create BMe with the Knight Foundation's support, I did so because I knew that black men like my grandfather, the brothers I met on the Mall in 1995, and those you see profiled in this book exist by the millions. I also knew that we were in a historic period of transition that allowed us to see that we didn't have to hold on to the death narratives of the baby-boom

generation. We could choose to define each other by our contri-
butions to society rather than by our costs or faults. We could
choose to look beyond birth characteristics like race and sex
toward our shared interests in prosperous communities.

As my sons' generation inherits the keys to the kingdom,
all bets are off for what the future holds. They are at a turning
point in the story of America, just as we were at the dawn of
integration. Back then, we were the face of a movement for
freedom. But somewhere along the way we let people mask us
as the face of poverty when they declared "War on Poverty,"
and the face of drugs when they declared "War on Drugs," and
now the face of crime as cities unite against crime. But this gen-
eration doesn't have to fall for that okey-doke. We are not the
majority of poor people, drug users, or criminals in America.
We are disproportionately engaged in creating businesses, serv-
ing our country, and supporting causes. That's who we are, and
that's who we are meant to be. If you do not define yourself,
then others will do it for you. As black men and as a nation, our
challenges are real, but our contributions are more real. What
you focus on has power over your life. So, as black males and
as Americans, we make our future when we make our choice.
Who do you *think* you are?

Shawn Dove

AGE: 52

TITLE: CEO, Campaign for Black Male Achievement

COMMUNITY: Harlem, NY

We need more people that unequivocally, without a doubt, love Black people. When you love Black people, you get obsessed about the work of elevating Black people. And nothing is going to change in this country until we have that critical mass of obsessed people. I believe we are approaching that tipping point.

I lead a national Campaign for Black Male Achievement for the Open Society Foundations. The campaign is a philanthropic strategy to improve the life outcomes for Black men and boys—a national movement to change the frame around how Black men and boys are perceived, how we value them, and how we invest in them. This is my life's work.

✦

I'm a native New Yorker—I've lived in all of the boroughs except Staten Island. I was born in 1962 to Deanna Cameron

and Bernard Dove, two dancers. They were never married and never lived together, so I don't have a memory of ever waking up and saying, "Good morning, Dad." My mother abandoned her artistic career and got a job in the federal government so she could support me. She worked in that role for thirty years.

Because my mom had to work so much, she knew I would need good guidance and care. I spent weekends with her in the Bronx, and days and nights during the week staying with my godmother, Lillian Smith, in Harlem. Lil, as we called her, was the classic den mama and also a towering figure in Harlem in the 1970s. She ran a boardinghouse that was always filled with colorful figures who were either living there or socializing there. She also ran numbers with Roy Barnes, the father of Nicky Barnes, a legendary Harlem hustler. It was like that in Harlem—everybody had a hustle, and good people did what they had to do to get by.

Lil had a huge apartment at 119th and Lenox Avenue, and besides me, she had a granddaughter and several other children who lived with her. These kids became my siblings. We weren't rich but I never felt poor. I felt loved. I was a part of an extended community that included Lil, my mom, my maternal and paternal grandparents, and the individuals in and around our Harlem community. If I did something wrong on 119th Street and Seventh Avenue I'd be reprimanded by someone who knew me as one of Lil's kids, and by the time I got back to Lenox Avenue I'd be reprimanded again. Then when I got back to Lil's apartment, she might be waiting for me with an ironing cord prepared to mete out some stern discipline.

✦

This extended family—blood relatives and friends—took an interest in me and became early guides as I navigated life. They also demonstrated the power of positive adult voices in a kid's

life. I still remember overhearing some adult at a party when I was six years old saying, "Shawn's a good reader. He likes to read." That built confidence in me—just those few words. It has stayed with me all these forty-six years later, and it's something that I'm very conscious of as I mentor people—the power of affirmative words.

After the fourth grade, my mom and I moved down to the Upper West Side in Manhattan and lived together full-time. She always made sure I was getting good exposure to good people and good experiences. I spent quality time with my paternal grandfather, Charner Dove. He was a carpenter who also loved horse racing. We spent many a summer Saturday afternoon at Aqueduct or Belmont. I observed his quiet confidence, experienced his gentle love of me. I also spent time with Lil's son, DeWitt Thompson, a Harlem hustler who believed in uplifting his community. Neither of these men conformed to the gender norm of being the strong, silent, inaccessible type. They offered a model of confidence and security, but they were also very loving, very nurturing.

My mother was also a stickler for education. Going into seventh grade, I was faced with the option of picking a major. It was either gym, which most Black and Latino students picked, or math and science, what mostly all the white students chose. I can remember opting for the gym track and bringing the form home for my mom to sign. Her reaction reflected her approach to raising me. "Oh no," she said. "You'd better go back and sign up for math and science." While my friends were playing sports, I was in the lab grudgingly learning about Bunsen burners and the like. But because of that choice, I was to attend one of the best high schools in New York City, Brooklyn Tech.

✦

Of course, the road was rocky at times, and my choices as a young person were often wrong. With my mom working as much as she did, I spent a lot of time alone. I started selling loose joints on the corner of 80th and Amsterdam when I was in middle school, just to make some money. My pitch was "Pass me by and you won't get high." I wasn't just selling weed, I was using weed, and drinking alcohol too. Eventually, I graduated to cocaine in my late adolescence.

It was around this time that some friends introduced me to The DOME Project. DOME stood for Development of Opportunities for Meaningful Education. It was a youth center run by a man named John Simon. John had a big beard and looked a bit like Charles Manson. I showed up hoping to score a free basketball jersey and sneakers, but I was struck by the cult-like atmosphere of the place. All of these young people were milling around asking John for help with their homework or advice on dealing with issues at home.

I started spending a lot of time at The DOME, eventually joining the basketball team. John coached the team, helped us improve our basketball skills, our teamwork, our character. But he was also adamant about us reading and, through reading, gaining a deeper sense of our own self-worth. Before games, we'd be in the locker room reading as a group out loud from *Manchild in the Promised Land*. Then we'd go out and play. Win or lose, I'd be back on the corner with my friends, selling loose joints, drinking a 40 of Old English, pretty much doing the wrong thing. But our conversations would be about *Manchild in the Promised Land*, so there were some subtle breakthroughs.

Like my grandfather and DeWitt, John exuded the self-assuredness and confidence we associate with the masculine ideal but also that warm, loving, nurturing side that is so important to helping young people feel supported. One day he pulled me aside. I thought he was not aware of my extra-

curricular activities at the corner of Eightieth and Amsterdam, but he was. "You have potential, Shawn," he said. "You can do something in life if you spend more time at The DOME and less time on the corner."

I began spending a lot more time there, and eventually I started youth organizing with The DOME. John helped me get a prep school scholarship to Lawrence Academy in Massachusetts, and twelve years later, at age twenty-four, I came back to work as The DOME's executive director. The year or so that I held the job was very stressful. Some people I was managing still saw me as "Little Shawn," and I was also still secretly struggling with my drug addiction. So I made the most transformational decision in my life thus far: I resigned, sought treatment, and I have been clean ever since.

◆

My work at The DOME helped launch my career in youth development, education reform, and community building. I realized that I had found my calling. In 1990, I joined the Harlem Children's Zone, and I worked for a decade with Geoffrey Canada—it was Geoffrey's predecessor, Richard Murphy, who hired me after I got clean. Then in 2006, I began a newspaper for Black fathers called *Proud Poppa*. The objective was to showcase everyday Black men who were being wonderful fathers to their children, pillars in their communities. It wasn't about the celebrity dads—it was based on the premise that there are Black fathers across this country who are heroes, whose stories don't make the news. What makes the news are stories of degradation and pain. But in order to combat the real issues that underlie those stories, we need to see those shining examples that we can all aspire to emulate—like the proud poppas.

I can't emphasize how important mentoring is for changing the game for Black males. Mentoring, for me, is about that

combination of instilling confidence and being nurturing. It's about revealing one's own vulnerabilities and failures as a basis for establishing genuine rapport with young people. It's about building that sense of belief in our youth. People will say we need to close the achievement gap, the education gap. This is true. But, to do so, we've got to close the belief gap—that's the self-belief Black males themselves have in their own worth, their own potential. It's also the belief society has in Black males.

The principles I impart to the many young people I've worked with over the years boil down to a few. First, we've got to be resilient. Life is going to deal us challenges and we have got to be able to bounce back. Second, be willing to be vulnerable. Be willing to put on the table what you're going through. Mentors can't be helpful if they don't know what's really going on. And third, really have a vision for your life that is not limited by your current circumstances. Allow yourself to dream, think about new ideas and possibilities, confront your fears, capture them in a journal, and then make "the ask" to those who can help you actualize yourself fully.

✦

Mentoring is not a one-way street. Many of the people I've mentored have in turn become mentors and sources of inspiration for me. One such person is Salahadeen Betts, who walked into *Harlem Overheard*, the youth newspaper we started as part of the Harlem Children's Zone. He was fourteen years old and had just witnessed his best friend, Mark, shot dead next to him on the street corner. He was a local graffiti artist from the Drew Hamilton projects whose tag was all over the walls in the neighborhood, and he was looking to turn his life around.

Salahadeen wanted to apply his graffiti skills to do illustrations for our paper. While he was working with us, he taught

himself HTML and various design programs. I could see his greatness and told him as much. Eventually he became the creative director of the paper. He finished high school, graduated from college, got married, now he's raising three kids. He discovered a talent for community organizing and youth organizing, and he has built a career serving young people in Harlem as the executive director of the Countee Cullen Community Center, which is housed in the elementary school he attended, and is the center I was directing when we first met.

I poured a lot into Salahadeen, but he's my hero because he's poured a lot into me—mostly, he's demonstrated the power of resiliency.

One of the things I always say is "There is nothing more powerful than the right word coming from the right person at the right time." I've experienced this truth throughout my life, and I believe it is vital to ensuring that African-American young men can truly realize their potential.

Frederick Hutson

AGE: 31

TITLE: President and CEO, Pigeonly

COMMUNITY: Las Vegas, NV

One of my strengths is also a weakness: I can see opportunity in just about anything. However, just because one can do something doesn't mean one should.

I've always been really handy; my passion is troubleshooting or fixing things. I was raised in Brooklyn and my parents divorced when I was young, so my siblings and I all did our part to keep the house moving forward. My mother, by necessity, was incredibly entrepreneurial—she had a job and supplemented her income by turning our living room into a restaurant so churchgoers would come to eat after their services.

Along with my two sisters and my brother, I did odd jobs around the apartment building for other tenants to contribute a few bucks to our household, be it fixing a refrigerator, a fan, or a light switch. I had a knack for fixing things; for hacking systems and putting them back together, better. I was always

the kid who had crazy ideas, big things that I wanted to build. My mother never stifled that.

When I was thirteen, we moved to St. Petersburg, Florida, to be near my mother's family. That was where I was introduced to the drug culture. The drug trade was all around me during my high school years. My cousins and their friends were selling, whether it was crack cocaine or marijuana.

I never got involved. But I had a close-up view of it. And I could see that there were inefficiencies in how people were operating—little things that could be fixed to make the whole process more profitable. Still, I stayed away from it—for the time being.

✦

Immediately after high school, I joined the air force. I was stationed in Las Vegas, and I was able to apply my technical skills to airplane mechanics, working on the electronic systems of the F-16 fighter jet. I learned discipline, how to work with people from different groups, how to motivate people, how to be a part of a much larger enterprise.

Still, my entrepreneurial spirit stuck with me. As soon as I arrived in Vegas and while I was on active duty, I decided I wanted to purchase a business. I became set on the idea that I would buy a gas station—everyone needs gas, so I figured I could make some good money owning one. But even with loans from the Small Business Administration, I found that I would still need to put down $120,000. It was way out of reach.

One day I saw a sign for a window-tinting company that had gone out of business. I knew nothing about window tinting, but I figured that this was something that people needed; Vegas is a hot place. I got with an air force buddy of mine, William, and we went into business. We hired some window

tinters, and within six months we grew the business from zero to $130,000 in sales. It was something I enjoyed doing—not because I enjoyed window tinting, but because I liked building and solving problems.

Soon afterward, we sold the business for a hefty sum. That was the first time I went from building something from scratch to selling it for a profit.

✦

In late 2004 some of my friends and family from Florida visited me in Vegas—including the cousins who were involved in the drug trade. At the time I was still active duty air force, and William and I had taken the profits from the window shop and invested in a retail cell phone store. I was still trying to make the $120,000 to buy a gas station.

My cousins and I got to talking, and at one point I mentioned something I'd observed while I was watching them in high school, the lack of efficiency in their drug operations. "You guys are moving product from Mexico to Arizona to Florida, which is a lot of stops and starts," I told them. "Meanwhile, the drugs are in your lap during the entire trip. This limits the total amount you can transport, and your risk of arrest is astronomically high." I suggested they use FedEx, UPS, and DHL to transport the product.

They liked the idea. And I still needed the $120,000 to buy my gas station. So I agreed to go into business with them.

We developed a system to mail marijuana from Nogales, Mexico, to Las Vegas. Basically, I would pick an address of some unsuspecting individual and ship the marijuana there. I didn't know them, they didn't know me. Meanwhile, I would pay off a courier for FedEx or UPS who had that address on their route. When the deliveryman reached the address, I would have an associate waiting outside to pick the package up.

If the police intercepted the package, they would talk to the person who lived at the address, who wouldn't know anything about it. So that person wouldn't go to jail, we wouldn't go to jail, and everybody would go home.

The system worked well for five years. I would receive the marijuana in Las Vegas and send it to Sarasota, Tampa, St. Petersburg—all around my cousins' territory in Florida. It was so successful that I bought a shipping store in Las Vegas so I could handle the interface with the shipping companies more effectively.

I was so naïve about the criminal justice system. I thought, if I don't get caught with anything, I can't go to jail. I didn't understand how conspiracy worked. I didn't understand how federal mail fraud worked.

What makes drugs such a stupid endeavor is that you can never deal with just yourself. You always have to deal with other people, and the more people who are involved, the more links that can break. One day in 2008 one of our Mexican connects got jammed up by police, and he named me and my cousins. A few days later I was standing outside of my shipping store, talking to customers. Five or six dark vans showed up, and eleven federal agents jumped out—FBI, ICE, DEA. I was arrested on conspiracy to distribute drugs. I ended up pleading out, and the judge sentenced me to fifty-one months in federal prison.

✦

I wouldn't recommend prison to anyone, but going to prison was actually good for me. It helped me to face the man I had become.

I realized that I had forgotten all about the reason I started selling drugs in the first place—to get the $120,000 to buy a gas station. I realized that I was being selfish: selling drugs not only hurts the people you love, it puts poison into the community.

I concluded that just because you can do something doesn't mean that you should do it.

I began reading the *Wall Street Journal* and any business book I could get my hands on. I became acquainted with the technical terms for things that I had learned in business either intuitively or by accident. I realized that I had been applying real business principles to my enterprises all along, both the legal and the illegal ones.

I also noticed something else: that the entire prison population was suffering from the same problem. It was very expensive for those of us on the inside to stay connected with friends and family on the outside. Beyond the feeling of emotional isolation, I saw that this had real consequences—it made it extremely difficult to be successful upon release, because you've lost the social and community connections with the people who would support you and help you get back onto your feet.

I started working on a business plan for how to address this problem.

◆

As soon as I was released, after fifty-seven months in prison and a halfway house, I began to execute my business plan with a friend from the air force, Alfonzo Brooks. Neither of us knew anything about software, but we pulled together our limited resources—$50 here, $100 there—to hire a freelance programmer and develop a prototype of what became Fotopigeon—a photo exchange site for prisoners and their families.

As a general rule, prisoners don't have access to the Internet and digital content. Fotopigeon allows family members to much more easily send digital photos in a hard copy form. When we created the prototype, I knew that the most efficient way to grow would be to market the product to the prison population and let it spread by word of mouth. Based on public

records, we developed a list of one hundred thousand prison inmates. We had a very limited budget, so we sent out greeting cards announcing our service to five hundred inmates from that list, suggesting they have their families visit our website.

The response rate was crazy: 25 percent of those who received the cards responded. Compare that to a typical response rate for a general market direct mailer, which is less than 1 percent. We knew we had something to build from. After six months, we had two thousand active users and we had shipped twenty or thirty thousand photos.

At the time we started, it was just Alfonzo and me. Now we've raised $2 million in seed funding, we have twelve full-time employees, we've shipped 150,000 photos, and we're still growing. Half of the prison population has a child under eighteen, so you can imagine how important it is to receive regular updates of photos from families on the outside.

We've also diversified our business and are working to solve another problem faced by inmates and their families: the exorbitant price of telephone calls. Our new service Telepigeon enables inmates and their families to communicate on a local telephone line. The result is an 80 percent reduction in the cost of calls, and we offer one hundred minutes of free talk time per month. Our goal is to ensure that cost isn't a barrier to prisoners remaining in contact with their families.

✦

We have a double–bottom line approach—we are a profit-driven company, but we also want to improve things for prisoners and society and are willing to give up some profit for the social mission.

The criminal justice system in America is about warehousing people, not rehabilitating them and preparing them to be productive citizens when they get out. Yet there are fifty thou-

sand people released back into society from prison each month. Many of these folks have spent significant periods of time in prison for nonviolent or first time offenses, often related to drug use or drug sales. I'm not condoning drugs and I believe that people need to be steered back into productive paths, but it's very clear to me that we're not correcting people and preparing them to be released—we're doing the opposite.

My experience in prison brought me face-to-face with the reality of isolation, and my enterprising nature, my technical gifts, my inclination to problem-solve, and my desire to help uplift our community led me to create Pigeonly. We still need significant criminal justice reform, but I hope that our work is a step in the direction of making things better. I'm proud to be applying my knack for fixing things to a business that is helping prisoners and their families and, in so doing, helping society.

Bill T. Jones

AGE: 62

TITLE: Cofounder, Bill T. Jones and
Arnie Zane Dance Company

COMMUNITY: New York, NY

I t was in the 1970s and my nephew and I were chatting as we drove through the Castro District of San Francisco. Full of a young child's enthusiasm and alertness, my nephew dropped his voice and said with as much authority as he could muster, "Uncle, these men here are gays!" "How can you tell?" I responded. "Because they all have beards. Gays always have beards."

"I don't have a beard," I cautiously added and waited as he struggled making sense out of this revelation. "Wow! I wanted to be just like you, but now . . . I have to think about it."

Recently I was having a phone conversation with this relative, now a man over forty struggling with chronic illness and a history of substance abuse. Our relationship over the years has ebbed and flowed. He did accept that he was a gay man, studied dance briefly, and had fleeting moments of success as a

dancer, singer, and model, but as he now confesses, he always maintained a "shadow life" of escape through drugs, sex, and excess. He feels the problems in his life are the results of choices his parents made, in particular his mother, who should have left his violent, drug-addicted father and fled with him and his four sisters. Careful not to discount my relative's feelings or rob him of his right to critique his present misery and the meaning of his life, I offered, "You certainly realize by now that we cannot really control other people's choices?"

✦

The conceiver of this book's project paid me a compliment by including me as one of the "black men of accomplishment" telling their stories. However, the two above-mentioned conversations with my nephew, separated by almost forty years, give me pause as I struggle with the notions of choice, behavior, and mentorship.

✦

My father, Gus Jones, was an enterprising man, and an entrepreneur. He used his strategic mind, his relationships, and the opportunities he perceived to create an independent business. In the 1940s, he recognized the opportunities associated with joining the stream of Southern field workers who followed the crops along the Eastern Seaboard. He and my mother decided to join what was then called "The Season" in the role of contractors of migrant laborers. They bought a battered school bus and a couple of old flatbed trucks, putting wooden sides and benches on them and covering them with tarpaulins. Single people and families who wanted to work in the North would pile into the bus and trucks and, after multiple stops harvesting fruits and vegetables on their way, reach New York's Finger Lakes district. In exchange for transport, room, and board, the

workers would pay a portion of their wages to my parents (who also worked the fields with them)—that was the business.

Seeing that self-contained community of people who were my color, striving for better lives against the odds—and seeing my father as the leader of that community—was an important message on a number of fronts. I came to understand the importance of self-sufficiency.

Through my father's example, I understood that there were certain codes that had to be switched on and off, depending on where and when one found oneself and to whom one was speaking. He was always ready with a smile, a funny story in dealing with all people, but in particular with the white farmers. I remember how everyone seemed to change and my father would move more slowly, deliberately choosing his words carefully, if for any reason the local police or state troopers showed up—be it on a Saturday morning or in the midst of a late Saturday night's "carrying on" as people were drinking, flirting, and dancing.

My father and mother, I am sure, were overwhelmed by the challenge of raising twelve kids without the benefits of education. My father received pay for the work from the farmers and turned it over to my mother, who managed the family's budget. In observing them, I learned that my mother and father were partners. Even though they fought a lot, he never struck her and she would refer to him in her Christmas prayer—which was a very important event—as her "helpmate." They were in this thing together!

✦

My dad's business went well for a few years, but with mechanization and the inflow of cheaper Hispanic workers, "The Season" was dying.

Gus Jones was determined to become a "Black Yankee." He

wanted his kids to have "the same opportunity as the white man's kids." Through education and by moving away from the Jim Crow South he believed we would have better prospects. So in 1955 we settled permanently in the Finger Lakes region of upstate New York.

This choice came with a price: loss of community and the cultural connections and traditions that informed it, as well as an ever-widening gap between the traditional, Southern worldview of my parents and the worldview developed by us, their children.

My parents did whatever it took to make this choice work, though they—my mother in particular—were uncomfortable with the mostly Italian and German families in our community.

My mother sent us, her children, to the local Methodist Church for services, but she herself would only attend, on significant occasions, a black church in Rochester, saying she "had no use for white preachers." And as day laborers/field workers and black people, my parents rarely came to our school's "pancake breakfasts" or PTA meetings.

However, if ever my mother felt we were being treated unfairly or slighted, a fierceness in her emerged. "C'mon! Stop crying! We gonna go and get to the bottom of this!" she'd say. We'd march down to the principal's office with her in the lead wearing her Sunday best, saying, "Just because my face is black, you can't treat my children like this!" That's a certain kind of fierceness—a fierceness that burns with determination, but also fear. A fear rooted in the harsh realities of race. A version of which I have seen in myself.

At school I learned early on that I could attract attention to myself by performing, clowning, telling risqué stories. Because I was one of a handful of blacks in the school and the only one in my class, it was assumed that I was naturally sexually precocious. Actually, I didn't have sex until I was seventeen,

unlike my older brothers, who bragged that they had had sex at eleven, twelve, or thirteen. I didn't understand sex and was quite panicked about it for reasons that would become clearer to me later. Over time, I came to understand that if I went to school every day, "spoke properly," and didn't air "black folks' business," I could fit in.

Or at least I thought I could. The senior prom, that age-old mating ritual, changed that. I invited a white female classmate whom I had known since kindergarten to be my date. Though it was spring of 1970—the era of Sidney Poitier's *Guess Who's Coming to Dinner?*—it certainly generated an uncomfortable community-wide discussion—one I could feel, though barely heard.

◆

That fall, I attended the State University of New York at Binghamton, where I soon dived into dance and the performing arts. It was in the wake of the civil rights movement and against the backdrop of the fraught and burgeoning counterculture. It was there that I met Arnie Zane.

Arnie was a Jewish-Italian man born in the Bronx. We cannot overestimate what it meant to me, at age nineteen, to meet another wounded but fierce human being who was living his own version of "We Shall Overcome." All his life he had been viewed as effeminate, literally fighting for his right to be. We fell in love and became partners, not just in life but—soon—in our life's work.

After a few years of experimentation at the American Dance Asylum, a progressive dance collective in Binghamton in 1978 we moved closer to NYC and became a duet team with an audacious plan: to start a dance company that reflected not just the color blindness that was supposed to characterize the counterculture of the time, but also the diversity of body

types—some tall, some short, some small, some large—which we ourselves had explored (Arnie was five-foot-four while I am six-one).

At the time, there were very few black choreographers in the "downtown" dance world. The mainstream dance world's expectation of me was that I would make works similar to Alvin Ailey's. Ailey was the most notable choreographer of color at the time. His work was rooted in the black American experience that is always shadowed by the "trauma narrative" of slavery and black oppression. But our approach was different. Yes, we too were talking about freedoms. The very sight of the two of us onstage, grappling and free associating, was its own type of protest.

Alvin looked at me and didn't see a threat; instead, I think he was proud. I was coming from a dance culture that didn't identify with what was called "Black Dance." I was making my reputation with a young white man. We were obviously a homosexual couple. Our choreography didn't conform to the expectation that audiences had that black men be men—that is, highly gendered. I represented something transgressive. Alvin offered me the opportunity to create two works for his company. And Artie and I brought Ailey on as a board member of our company. Having his name on the letterhead was a profound endorsement and for this I'll be always grateful.

✦

In 1983 I was working on one of the pieces I made for Alvin's company, a rough, athletic romp called "Fever Swamp." Some of the choreography was physically dangerous. He attended one of the rehearsals and leaned over, saying with a smile, "Bill, don't you hurt my boys!"

This moves me to this day. I know what he meant. He was "a black gay man." He had travails "looking for love in

all the wrong places." But this was not what motivated his admonition. He knew he was the first black male to gain real recognition and acceptance in the broader contemporary dance community. He had the generosity to reach out and help others. He was a nurturer. When he said, "my boys," it communicated that the dancers in his company, most of whom were black, were his charges. They were precious enough young men that they should be treated with care.

There is an insidious perception among some that black males are dumb animals, prized for some elemental skill but also expendable. You can see this in athletics and pornography. It was an important lesson for me to hear Alvin Ailey—someone who had achieved an elevated status in his field—so clearly articulate genuine care and affection for these young men.

His words remind me of a quote by a friend and mentor of mine, filmmaker Marlon Riggs, the creator of a seminal documentary titled *Tongues Untied*. In the film, Riggs argues that one of the most radical things that black people can do is to love black men. He meant it in the context of male/male love, but by extension he was saying it's okay to love blackness, to love black bodies, for black men to love black men. Like Alvin Ailey said, "Don't you hurt my boys!"

I agree!

✦

For me, it comes down to this: Can I love the place that I come from? Can I not be ashamed of poverty, of having been a field worker, of my father having failed in his dream? And as a choreographer, as an elder statesman in dance, can I love the young people in general—men and women—who are my charges? Do I have integrity? Do I have a "worth ethic"? Do I honor my relationship(s)? Do I dare do the things that for too many years we have been told that black men do not do?

Color blindness is complicated. As I've become older, I have found it less appealing. I want to be very clear that I honor, respect, and love all of the dancers in my company irrespective of gender or race. They are all my charges. But I am concerned with the young black people and feel more clearly that I have a special responsibility to them.

So, what is the challenge facing young black men and how do we address it? Many young black men grow up in households without fathers. It says a couple of things: One, that Dad's full of shit, he doesn't love me, that Dad cannot be trusted. Two, that black men are expendable. They are not really builders of families; in fact, they pose a threat to the family.

You must choose to counter this framing of black men. You must choose a fierce commitment to being builders. Taking Malcolm X and Martin Luther King as examples, can you choose not to fear conflict and resoluteness? Can you choose to live "free at last" as a verb—as an action?

As I said to my relative, "You certainly realize by now that we cannot really control other people's choices?" . . . But we can control our own!

Reverend Al Sharpton

AGE: 60

TITLE: President and Founder, National Action Network

COMMUNITY: New York, NY

People think I was born in the 'hood, but that's not quite right. Early in life I lived in a four-family house in a mixed neighborhood in Brooklyn. My father owned a corner store, and over the period of my adolescence he bought twenty apartment buildings and a construction company. We moved to Hollis, Queens, when I was four, and he used to buy a Cadillac every year. We were upwardly mobile.

Then when I was nine and a half, my family was torn apart. My father had an affair with my stepsister from my mother's first marriage, and he abandoned us. We moved back to Brooklyn, first to a housing development and then to Brownsville, where my mother had to make it on welfare as a domestic worker.

The one consistent element during this time of upheaval was the church. My parents attended Washington Temple Church of God and Christ, which was probably the first Pentecostal

megachurch in New York. They had about three thousand members, and the pastor was Bishop F. D. Washington, named after Frederick Douglass.

Bishop Washington was a major figure in religious circles. He had a gospel TV show that they filmed in the church, so all the big gospel artists came through. I would come home from Sunday morning services and put on my mother's nightgown and act like it was a minister's robe. He used to have bags under his eyes, so I would draw circles under my eyes. And I could preach almost verbatim what Bishop Washington preached at Sunday services.

Bishop Washington encouraged all of it. He had started preaching as a boy himself, so he let me preach my first sermon when I was literally four years old. He was the one who coined my nickname, the "Boy Wonder Preacher." He let me form a junior church, where I was the junior pastor, I had a junior usher boy, a junior choir, a junior trustee. All of us were between four and ten years old, but it was his way of nurturing and giving us leadership and responsibility.

✦

After my father left our home, I found another mentor in Reverend Walter Banks. Reverend Banks was a minister at Washington Temple, and he sort of took me in. He was a voracious reader, and he would take me to a bookstore on Fifth Avenue called Brentano's, and we would spend every Saturday there buying books and talking about books. The next week he'd test me to make sure I read them. He also started taking me on weekend excursions and showing me all these different things in life that I'd never imagined. He brought me to the Four Seasons, and he'd say, there's another kind of life—this is what you need to aspire to.

When I was around eleven years old I became fascinated

with Adam Clayton Powell. I used to shop for books in a black-owned bookstore in Hollis, Queens, across the corner from my school. I remember seeing this one book that had a guy on it who looked like a white guy with a clergyman's collar. It was Adam Clayton Powell. I bought the book—it was 99 cents, and I had a little bit of money because I'd get little offerings of five or ten dollars from preaching.

I read the book, and I couldn't look away. Here was this preacher that also had enormous political power, and that would lead these movements. I found out that Reverend Powell had helped Bishop Washington get the mortgage for the church that I grew up attending.

I started to beg my mother to let me go to Harlem to meet Reverend Powell. She told me that Harlem was dangerous, but after a few months she gave in and took me up on the number two train to hear his sermon.

I will never forget that sermon. It has been decades, and I can still see him out on that pulpit; I've never been more impressed than I was that morning. After he finished preaching, I went to the back of the church to find him—by this point, I had navigated enough churches to know how to find the pastor's study. I knocked on his office door and his secretary answered. It was one of those doors that open halfway up, and she could barely see me, I was so short. She asked who I was, and I told her, "I'm Reverend Alfred Sharpton, and I'd like to see Reverend Powell."

At first she just laughed—I think she was stunned by my forwardness. But eventually she led me to him. He was changing clothes, talking with some of the mothers of the church. When I walked in he turned around and said, "So this is the boy preacher from Brooklyn, Alfred Sharpton." He had heard me on my radio broadcasts. He put on his clergy collar and a jacket, and invited me to the Red Rooster for a cigar and a drink—in my case a Coca-Cola.

From then on, every time Reverend Powell was in town, I would go to Harlem and just follow around behind him. I would sit up and watch him in the restaurants. Sometimes he'd let me ride downtown when he was doing a TV show. Everywhere he went, people would mob him and he would talk this strong black protest talk. I learned from him, and I started to develop a political consciousness.

✦

In 1968 Martin Luther King was killed. I went to see a film about King's speech "Where Do We Go from Here?" I remember during the movie hearing the song "Why? (The King of Love Is Dead)," and I felt like Nina Simone was singing it to me. I went and I told my friends that I was going to be active in politics like Reverend Powell.

I organized my first campaign in 1969, when Reverend Powell was being pushed out of Congress by his peers. I put together a youth committee to support him, composed of kids from the various churches in the community. He was ultimately defeated by Charlie Rangel in 1970, but I wasn't done with activism. I kept getting involved, leading marches at my school, mostly antiwar because Vietnam was raging.

At first, Bishop Washington was concerned that I was leaning away from the church. Mostly, he didn't want me to get involved with the Black Panthers or other militants that he saw as "radicals." So with the blessing of my mother, Bishop Washington introduced me to Bill Jones, the leader of a civil rights organization that Dr. King had started called Operation Breadbasket. He said, if Alfred is going to be a social activist, at least he'll stay in the church.

Operation Breadbasket was where I met Jesse Jackson. I was thirteen years old and already serving as youth director of New York Breadbasket; Jesse was in his late twenties and was the

national director. He had a big Afro, and instead of a necktie he wore these big buckskin vests and a King medallion. He reminded me of Reverend Powell in his flamboyance.

When we met, Bill Jones introduced us, and he asked Jesse, "Do you have any advice for young Alfred?" And Jesse said, "Be careful, choose your targets carefully, do your research, and kick ass."

I was stunned; I had never heard a preacher curse before. So Jesse became my new Reverend Powell. And instead of just hanging out in his entourage, I actually worked with him. I learned the tactics, how to organize and how to move people.

✦

When I was sixteen years old I struck out on my own. Jesse had a major falling out with the Southern Christian Leadership Conference (SCLC) and left to start Operation PUSH in Chicago. I formed my own youth group in New York City to do many of the things we did at Breadbasket—try to get summer jobs for kids, voter registration, and the like. I had support from the black political and business leaders I knew from my time with Breadbasket—Bayard Rustin donated my first $500—and within a year I had my own radio show and everything. There were news articles in the *New York Times* and all of that—the boy preacher starting his own youth group.

One of the guys who joined my youth group was Teddy Brown, who came to New York from Georgia. Soon enough I found out he was James Brown's son. I had a lot of affection for James Brown; my father would bring me and my sister to the Apollo to see him perform. Teddy and I got close, and when he was killed in a car crash a few months later, his father reached out to me about putting on a show in honor of his son. That started a gradual relationship where he became like the father I never had.

You know, a lot of books and articles say I was James Brown's road manager. That's not true. I never worked for him; he wouldn't let me work for him. When I was on the road with him, he would tell his manager to give a donation to my youth group instead of paying me directly; he didn't want it said that I ever worked in entertainment. He wanted me to stay in civil rights and the church.

✦

I started the National Action Network in 1991, and my dream was always to build an organization along the lines of Operation Breadbasket and Operation PUSH—a church-based social action group. Today we have about seventy chapters and regional offices across the country.

Some years ago I decided that I wanted to offer the same thing to young men as my mentors offered to me. If James Brown and Jesse and Bill Jones hadn't spent time with me, I probably never would have done what I'm doing—I wouldn't have known how.

A lot of my chapter leaders are in their twenties and thirties, and many of them are young men. Many come from single parent homes, though some come from solid homes and have no connection to the streets. I spend a lot of time with them. I call it "time in action." I tell them, if you want to learn, then pack your bags. Go on the road with me, and read this book and that book on the plane. I feel like Reverend Banks.

Still, there's a difference between being a student of someone and becoming a clone. I caution the young men against mimicry, and I tell them, develop your own style. Learn some basic skills from me and do it your way, because in your generation, in your time, you will need different skills. People respect people that are authentic, and if you just copy me, people will see that.

Out of all my guys—and there are women too—I don't know who will be the next president, who will be the next big leader. One thing I learned from my predecessors, a mistake I saw my mentors make, is that you can't choose your successors. You can only give everybody a shot and let the water seek its own level.

I turned sixty years old in October. I'm trying in the next few years to pass the leadership of NAN on to somebody else. James Brown said something to me once that I'll never forgot. He said, "Rev, always remember that you get good days, and some days last longer than others. But when it's time to move on, it's better for you to get off the stage with people saying, 'Man, I wish Al was here,' than to stay on the stage so long that people say, 'I wish he'd get off.'"

Alfred Liggins III

AGE: 50

TITLE: President and CEO, Radio One, Inc.

COMMUNITY: Silver Spring, MD

I'm the president and CEO of Radio One, Inc., the only African-American-owned multimedia company serving the African-American community through the radio (Radio One and Reach Media), television (TV One), and digital (Interactive One) platforms. My mother, Cathy Hughes, and my then stepfather, Dewey Hughes, started this company in 1980. I was fifteen years old at the time, so I literally grew up in the business.

I still remember the excitement we felt when my family took over WOL-AM in Washington, DC, at midnight on October 3, 1980. It was the dawning of a new era, a chance for my parents to realize their dreams. They had worked for others in the local media for years and, while attempting to buy their first radio station, even tried promoting a local club. They weren't afraid to work while they saved and identified the resources necessary

to purchase a station. And one day, at the stroke of midnight, Radio One was born.

The first five years were rough. They shouldered high interest rates, lost money, and nearly went out of business. They were an AM signal, and there were larger stations on the FM dial in our area, like WHUR at Howard University and WKYS, owned by NBC. Both stations were major players in attracting African-American music listeners. In general, those were the stations that everyone was listening to. Our little AM station had about a 1 percent market share.

✦

That 1 percent franchise was due in large part to my mother's efforts. She hosted a morning show and she was able to carve out a niche as the "voice of the Black community." She became quite well known around Washington, DC, and had a powerful grassroots following. There were enough people who listened to my mother's show and would patronize our advertisers that it allowed us to turn that little AM station into a business that could hold its own.

I joined the business in 1985, when I was twenty years old. I was the sales rep that was never going to jump ship for a larger station. My mother was my first teacher. She taught me the radio business—about serving listeners and advertisers. She also gave me general lessons in business about what it takes to succeed. She demonstrated tenacity, perseverance, and showed me how to manage a tight budget.

I remember her waking me up in the morning when I was a sales rep, saying, "Get out of bed. You've got to collect this money from the hair care company because we have payroll coming up. Get over there and sit in their lobby until they give you a check."

✦

One of the biggest sources of guidance and support to me over the years has been Terry Jones. Terry is a partner at Syndicated Communications Venture Partners (Syncom), the private equity company that backed my parents in the acquisition of WOL-AM. He's the one who taught me the acquisition business.

With Terry's support of $7.5 million, we bought our first FM radio station, WMMJ, in 1987. My mother, Terry, and I worked to secure the financing and structure the deal. It was a tremendous learning experience and piqued my interest in the capital markets part of the business.

That was really the start of our upward trajectory. AM radio was being surpassed by the quality of music on the FM dial. With our first FM station we essentially started a new format— urban adult contemporary—which boiled down to "Motown and more." There was nothing like it yet on the East Coast—at least nothing that was aimed at African-Americans over the age of thirty-five. It was an instant hit.

From there, the story of our company has been one of growth and expansion. Five years after buying WMMJ-FM, in 1992, we were billing $10 million and turning $5 million in profit. From there we purchased two radio stations in Baltimore and in 1993 acquired one of our primary competitors in that market.

Nineteen ninety-five was a watershed year for us. We bought our biggest competitor in the Washington, DC, market, WKYS. I started a separate company and bought WHTA-FM in Atlanta. The timing was right for edgy hip-hop and those stations really took off. After several years, all of our stations were generating healthy profits.

✦

Terry Jones was with me as I structured these acquisitions, helping me to strategize our approach, secure our capital, and grow

the business. Terry gave me my real first insight into both the financial and capital markets sides of the business.

Working with Terry gave me the confidence to start thinking more expansively about larger radio stations and to think about tapping into the public capital markets. I developed relationships with large banks and ultimately began looking into what it would take to have an initial public offering and be listed on a stock exchange. I looked around at some larger, well-established companies that were doing much larger transactions, and I made the decision then that I wanted to be a public company. I wanted to own a big piece of a public company and grow it long-term.

In May of 1999, we did just that. When we went public, I was with my mom, several family members, and associates on the Credit Suisse trading floor. The stock opened at $28 and less than an hour later it was at $30. It was amazing to watch it trade up and up. Later that day my mom, grandmother, aunt, uncle, and I were walking the streets of New York taking it all in, and we walked by a ticker on the outside of a building. We saw ROIA (our ticker symbol) go by and it read $35. It was a euphoric time, a defining moment.

With access to the public markets we suddenly had the resources to invest in our expansion. We invested more than $1.2 billion in buying radio stations across the country, and we expanded our portfolio significantly. In 2004, we created and launched TV One. It's a successful business that turned a profit ahead of schedule.

✦

We've had our ups and downs. When the whole financial world came crashing down in 2008, I was concerned and uneasy. Banks that had made money off of us for years were calling in their loans. Our stock price hit 6 cents. I had to kick into

overdrive with financial reengineering to ensure that we stayed afloat and positioned ourselves for growth down the road.

That experience reminded me how critical our relationship with the African-American community is to our existence and how supportive the Black community is to its own. Radio One and TV One would not exist if the Black community didn't want them to. When we've sought help from members of the Black community, we've received it, and people have said, "I'm happy to help. Cathy Hughes helped me out twenty years ago." When we've run into opposition, the audience has come out in support; the clergy, members of Congress, and leaders of much larger corporations have all looked out for us.

I'll never forget the way Dick Parsons, then chairman and CEO of Time Warner, advocated for TV One to be delivered on Time Warner Cable. He told his cable system executives that we provide quality programming and address a need in the market. That was a game changer for us.

We've spent the last few years stabilizing the business, and I am proud of how far we've come from the dark times of the financial crisis.

We've built our business to serve the African-American community and we have benefited from that service; so we have a responsibility to be good stewards in the community. That reciprocal relationship has always been critical to our success. We have a real responsibility to the community and we take it seriously.

A big part of that is helping to turn around the narrative on African-American males. This means continuing to show role models of folks who are doing it a different way, who are helping each other, who are building their communities.

My mother and people like Terry Jones have been incredible role models for me in that they are sharp businesspeople who recognize that their business success is rooted in their relation-

ship with the Black community. I've emulated this understanding and put it into action in my own life. I believe that we have a responsibility as a media organization to shed light on the positive things that are happening in our community, to grow with our community, and to be responsive to its aspirations. This is how we've always done it. And this is how we will continue to build our legacy.

Emmett D. Carson, PhD

AGE: 55

TITLE: President and Chief Executive Officer, Silicon Valley Community Foundation

COMMUNITY: Silicon Valley, CA

When I was in third grade, maybe seven or eight years old, a young man was shot in the head right outside of my family's home in Chicago. He was the son of our neighbor. He had gone to the store to pick up milk. My mom and I hunkered under a picture window as bullets shattered it, while my father, my hero, a World War II veteran, went out and dragged the young man into our house. The young man survived, but was never the same.

We left the neighborhood shortly after the incident. This was 1967. We moved thirty blocks away, farther south to an upper middle class neighborhood called Chatham Village. It was a solidly Black community—Mahalia Jackson owned a home around the corner, one of the Black city council members lived across the street, and there were many doctors and lawyers. I had a basketball hoop in the backyard over the garage. We had "moved on up."

My world changed. I could ride my bike as far as I wanted to without fear of it being stolen. I was in a public school where my teachers had expectations that I would succeed and go off to college.

In an odd way, this new life only gave me a sense of added obligation. I had moved thirty blocks, and all of a sudden everything was in front of me—I was told that every opportunity could be mine if I worked for it. And yet I had friends and family in the old neighborhood who were not going to be exposed to the same things—who in fact were being told that they did not have those same opportunities. These friends were equally as capable as I was in every respect, but they still had to live with the violence and the low expectations. I achieved freedom, and yet my friends and family remained trapped in a modern day socioeconomic slavery. I had the bittersweet feeling of having escaped and at the same time having left people behind.

The unfairness of it all shaped me, and continues to shape me to this day.

✦

At a very young age I was told that I was adopted. I didn't look anything like either of my parents, and when I was very young, the neighborhood kids would tease me by telling me that I wasn't my parents' child. It turned out to be true.

When my parents told me about my adoption, they made sure to emphasize that I was wanted; I was chosen. My adoptive father reminded me that they had given me his name, Emmett. That had a transformative effect on me. I knew I wasn't an accident—I was part of the family and I was a child that they loved. At the same time, it put a big burden on me. I felt that since I was "chosen," then I had to show them that they had made a good choice.

Growing up, I was the kid who would get As and Bs, but the

teacher would tell my parents I could do better. That all changed in freshman year of high school. There was a young lady I was attracted to who had a very strict mom. After school her mom would only let her go to the library to study. So the only way I was going to find time to talk to her was if I went to the library.

Lo and behold, when I was in the library I couldn't talk a whole lot, because the librarians were walking around hushing us. So I actually had to study. I started reading everything, fully absorbing things. I came back to school in sophomore year, and I found out that I had been put in an academic "section" with all the smart kids. I knew who the geeks were, and I'd been placed with the geeks.

I did well enough to get a full ride to Morehouse. I graduated early, was accepted into Princeton—in the middle of the year—which, I'm told, they had never done before. I earned my master's and PhD in four and a half years. In part, I credit that girl whose mom made her go to the library. So the lesson is, if you're a guy, get attracted to somebody smart whose mom makes her go to the library. I know that's old school, but it works.

✦

Throughout my career, I've always tried to ask myself the same question—if I'm in a seat of authority, am I using that seat to make a difference in people's lives? Will things be different because I occupied the chair?

By 1989, I was at the Ford Foundation, working as a program officer. There'd been a number of street shootings that year, many involving innocent people. In fact, there was this one particularly horrendous shooting in which a woman was killed walking with her toddler on the way to return a VHS tape to the video store—she was basically targeted by a sniper. Knowing my background, it isn't surprising that this really affected me.

At the time, the Ford Foundation didn't have any program

at all dealing with urban violence or gun control. Now, I knew that the then president of the foundation, Susan Berresford, always came in early in the morning. If you got in early enough, you could get to her before the support staff guards were able to block your way. Still, very few people had the nerve to walk right in like that—you did so at your own risk.

One morning shortly after the shooting, I came in early and walked into Susan's office. I put the *New York Times* front page on her desk and said, "Have you read this?" She said, "Yes, it's terrible." She told me what I already knew, that we didn't have a program in that area. That diminutive response was unacceptable to me. I said, "This kid saw his mother get assassinated. We're the Ford Foundation. We should be doing something about this."

At that point Susan told me, "Okay, Emmett, you're right. What would you have us do?"

I didn't have an answer for her. So she said, "I'll make you a promise. Come back to me with a fully formed plan of what we might do, and I'll figure out if it's a good plan, and whether we can do it."

In three or four weeks I came back with an outline of what we could do and how we could get involved, consistent with the Ford Foundation's values and perspectives. Susan gave me the money that we needed and said, "This is now an added part to your portfolio." I've always admired Susan for hearing me out, for letting me vent a little bit, and then giving me a chance to make a difference.

◆

This willingness to take a risk for the sake of authenticity is crucial to making meaningful change. After working at Ford I was hired as CEO of the Minneapolis Foundation in Minnesota in 1994. I was thirty-three years old. I made an effort to bring my

early experiences of empathy to the position, even if it meant taking on risks.

One of the most controversial things we did was also something that I am most proud of. There was a young man in Minneapolis who had been shot and killed. He was a gangbanger. We went to his mother and asked for her permission to take a photo of him in his casket, and she said yes. We created a brochure featuring the photo of the young man in his casket along with facts about how violence was destroying that community. That summer the brochure was widely credited with helping to save lives. A lot of young people out on the street had known the victim, and the photo helped make them realize that death was real and final.

Another project we took on was reinstating voting rights for ex-felons in Minnesota. According to state law, there was a provision that once you served your time you should be able to vote. But in reality, there was no process for getting your voting rights reinstated. There was a process to take you off the voting rolls, but no process to get you back on the rolls. We funded a study about the issue, which encouraged the state to establish a process through which convicted felons who had served their time could have their voting rights reinstated.

We took a lot of heat for that. I would talk about the disenfranchisement of felons and people would say, well, they should not have broken the law. I would explain that in Minnesota, if you caused $500 worth of damage from graffiti, or if you broke into a car, that was a felony. So if you committed this crime at seventeen, and you had served your time, should you never be allowed to vote again?

The grant to fund that study only cost us about $20,000. It wasn't about the money, or the size of our foundation—it was about the question—were we willing to take on tough and often controversial issues from a position of authenticity?

✦

I think the sense of unfairness that I experienced early in life still drives me to this day. I'm still struck by the question, What is it about a system in which you can move one person thirty blocks into a completely gang-free and violence-free external environment and change that person's life's trajectory? Why was I lucky enough to have this happen to me?

I came to the Silicon Valley Community Foundation in 2006 because I was looking for a challenge. The foundation advances innovative philanthropic solutions to challenging problems, engaging donors to make our region and world a better place for all. I was looking to do something that no one had ever done before, which was to merge two large community foundations: Peninsula Community Foundation and Community Foundation Silicon Valley. The smart money said it wouldn't work, but the board and staff made it work.

We started at $1.4 billion in assets, and fast-forward eight years, we're over $5 billion in assets. We're the largest community foundation in the world, and the largest grant maker in the nine-county San Francisco Bay Area. We're also fifteenth largest international funder in the United States. Moving forward, one of our strategic goals is to master how we can use the technology from Silicon Valley in the service of social justice.

We don't yet have a society where we can say that success is random. Success is determined by your zip code, by your race and ethnicity, and by your parents' wealth status. Recognizing that some people are going to be smarter than others and some people are just going to be luckier, I want everyone to have a fair shot. Within those two boundaries, everybody should have an equal opportunity to succeed.

Rev. Dr. Joseph Lowery

AGE: 93

TITLE: Founder, Joseph E. Lowery Institute; President, Southern Christian Leadership Conference, 1977–1997

COMMUNITY: Atlanta, GA

M y parents were very strong role models for me growing up. My father was a businessman, though he had limited formal training. My mother was a schoolteacher. They were both very caring and they took great pains to raise their children.

I was born in Huntsville, Alabama, but my parents did not want me growing up there. This was the 1920s and 1930s, after all, so the schools in Huntsville were segregated by race. My parents were not satisfied with the education I would be getting, so they sent me to Chicago to live with a friend of my father's and go to school there.

I would come back to Alabama during the summers. My father had a store he called "The Sweet Shop," and I would often work there. One afternoon when I was around twelve years old I was walking out of the store when this big burly policeman approached me in the doorway. The policeman was white; there

weren't any black policemen in Alabama back then. I was two-thirds of the way out, and he took his club and punched me back. He said, "Get back, nigger. See the white man coming?"

I was furious. As soon as the policeman left me, I went back home and went to my father's room, to the drawer where I knew he kept his pearl-handled pistol. Back in those days, I wasn't committed to nonviolence.

Strangely enough, right at that moment my father came home. I don't ever remember seeing him home at that time of day before, but he showed up, and he immediately sensed that something was wrong. He discovered that I had the gun, and he beat the devil out of me for thinking that violence was the solution.

The following day my father went to the mayor of our town to complain about the behavior of the policeman. The mayor said there wasn't anything he could do about it. That policeman was the only kind of white man he could hire. I decided then that I had to play a role in changing the climate of the nation. But I had learned from my father that violence was not the way to accomplish it.

✦

When I was nearing thirty I was called to the ministry. I felt that God was calling me, and I answered. I was ordained in 1950 as a minister in the United Methodist Church and I've been a pastor-preacher ever since.

I was pastor of the Warren Street Methodist Church in Mobile, Alabama, from 1952 through 1961. After Rosa Parks was arrested for refusing to give up her bus seat to a white passenger, the black community in Mobile was inspired to take action, and I became president of the Alabama Civic Affairs Association. Our goal was to continue the momentum and keep protesting for the desegregation of buses and public places. Just

like my father taught me, I stayed committed to the principles of nonviolence.

Dr. Martin Luther King Jr.—or Martin, as I call him—was a mentor, particularly in the context of reminding me of the value of nonviolence. I first met Martin at Boston University, where he was a graduate student and was attending a three-day workshop. When I was in Mobile he moved to nearby Montgomery, and we struck up a friendship through our work in Alabama.

I looked up to Martin as a pastor, and I admired his stewardship of the movement. We formed the Southern Christian Leadership Conference (SCLC) together and remained friends until he died in 1968. He was a wonderful man—probably the most interesting figure I've ever known.

SCLC was a great movement. I call it a movement because it was more movement than organization. We never had the organized structure that the NAACP had. And we didn't want it. We supported the NAACP, loved the NAACP, many of us came out of the NAACP, but we didn't want to be the NAACP. They were legal action; we were direct action. And that's the way we liked it.

I'm not sure if there was ever one moment when I knew I could be a leader. Even with the SCLC, I came up through the ranks. I was vice president, then chairman of the board, and then president for twenty years, from 1977 to 1997. I was president for longer than Martin and Ralph Abernathy put together. I don't know if that's because they couldn't get anyone else to take the job.

✦

In 2001, the Joseph E. Lowery Institute for Justice and Human Rights at Clark Atlanta University was founded. The mission of the institute is to provide a platform for citizens of every walk

of life to learn the important principles that underlie nonviolent advocacy. We aim to teach future leaders and "change agents"—including students in grade school—about temper control, about anger control, and about race conciliation.

Simply put, our mission is to change lives for the better in a real and permanent way.

My youngest daughter, Cheryl, is now the executive director of the institute. We had a good year last year. Through our in-school violence initiative we annually award fourteen fellowships to undergraduate students in the metropolitan Atlanta area. We call our fellows "Change Agents" and they receive training and certification that incorporate conflict resolution, peer mediation, mentoring, and nonviolent principles of learning and social action. The Change Agents work directly with elementary school students four days a week throughout the school year in order to teach and model nonviolent methods to deal with conflict and anger.

The impact that our Change Agents have on the children is remarkable. As one young brother told one of the fellows at our end-of-the-year program, "I didn't want to fight, I just didn't know what else to do."

We have also started giving out the Agent of Change Award. Tyler Perry received the first award this past October. He is a remarkable man who took what God gave him and changed the landscape of an industry that shunned him. He is a Change Agent in his respective field and in our country.

✦

Since my time working with Martin, everything has changed and nothing has changed. We've got more black policemen and black chiefs, and yet we have racial profiling from police. Black men today are still scapegoats. Black men have been abused, misused, they have been the butt of jokes.

Still, we are just now coming into a new era of black male leadership that I'm very proud of—men like Ben Jealous and Martin Luther King III. It's a new age and I'm very proud of the role that black men play.

I've seen a lot of changes. And I'm proud of the changes that have been made. I'm hoping that we'll continue to improve race relations. And I think we will. We're going to get there.

Ten or fifteen years after the incident with the police officer in my childhood, I was pastoring a church in Birmingham and I heard that the same officer was now a pastor, and he was pastoring a church in nearby Huntsville. And while I was standing there on the porch, he approached me with the mayor. I recognized him right away. My mother became nervous; she didn't want me to recognize him. But he came right up to me and said, "Are you Joe?"

Just to be sure, I said, "Yes, who are you?" And he told me he was the policeman who had brutalized me.

I said, "I understand you're in the ministry." He said, "Yes, so are you." I had never really forgiven him for what he did, because there was no justification for it. But I said to him, "Well I guess forgiveness is the order of the day."

The Lord's Prayer reminds us to forgive us our trespasses as we forgive those who trespass against us. If we don't forgive, then we can't reap forgiveness . . . the heart and soul of faith is the willingness to forgive and to be forgiven.

Reverend Raphael Warnock

AGE: 45

TITLE: Senior Pastor, Ebenezer Baptist Church

COMMUNITY: Atlanta, GA

I am the senior pastor at Ebenezer Baptist Church in Atlanta, Georgia, spiritual home of the Rev. Dr. Martin Luther King Jr. Dr. King was the grandson and son of Ebenezer's second and third pastors, and here he served alongside his father, Martin Luther King Sr., from 1960 to 1968. All of them were activist preachers. For them, the whole community, indeed the world, was their parish. Inspired by that rich tradition and informed by the mentorship of others, I have sought humbly to do my own work, as Ebenezer's fifth pastor in a legacy of justice-making ministry and service that began in 1886.

I was born in a blended family of twelve children. I am child number eleven, the youngest of seven boys. Both my mother and father were Pentecostal preachers in Savannah, Georgia, so I grew up in an environment that placed great value on personal piety. I was raised in a family and small church community of

people who saw God in the mundane and who lived their toilsome lives with profound gratitude for every blessing and evidence of God's presence with them in struggle and victory.

I have often joked that my parents spoke to me every day in King James English. That is to say that, with seriousness and regularity, they interpreted the meaning of their life experiences through Scripture. Faith-filled people, they were also practical people, who believed you should work like the outcome depends completely on you and pray like it depends ultimately on God.

My father was my first hero. During the week, he was a junk man. He picked up old junk cars on a rig that he constructed himself, and fixed the cars for resale. He had served in the army during World War II, where he learned mechanics and welding. On Sundays, my dad would put on his Sunday best and preach at a small holiness church in Savannah. Preacher and pastor to ordinary working class people, he put more money in the offering plate than they could ever afford to pay him. But he remained faithful. He was a preacher and a businessman—a junk man who recycled old broken cars from Monday to Saturday and spoke about a God—"a junk man" who loved the forgotten and marginalized—to broken people on Sunday morning.

I admired my father's strength and stamina, his personal integrity, and his commitment to community. I admired his ability to inspire people in the pulpit on Sundays. He was a small man in physical stature, but he was strong physically, socially, and spiritually.

Early one Sunday morning when I was six years old, my father was struggling, as pastors sometimes do, with what to include in his sermon later that morning. I heard him say to himself, "What am I going to say to God's people this morning?" He didn't realize that I was listening, but I was, and I piped up, "Dad, I'll preach for you this morning." I'd been practicing my

revival preaching by watching my father and some of the fiery Pentecostal preachers who would come through Savannah. I wasn't quite ready at six, but in fact I did start preaching by age eleven.

<center>✦</center>

I had this role model right in front of me, but I also became enamored of another man that I never knew, a man who had died one year before I was born—Martin Luther King Jr. I was very much attracted to Dr. King's power as a preacher, as a spokesperson for justice. I was moved by his ability to inspire people to risk their lives for the sake of a larger purpose.

In a real way, Dr. King recruited me to Morehouse. I first learned about the school through a story about Dr. King's student days there, where he read Henry David Thoreau's essay on civil disobedience. I researched further and discovered this incredible tradition of the school training Black men, leaders, spiritual leaders. I decided that Morehouse was where I should attend college.

I may not have gotten to Morehouse if I hadn't been a participant in the Upward Bound program at Savannah State University for my four years in high school. Upward Bound simplified the college application process, helped me access the grants and guaranteed loans I would need to pay for college, and enabled me to take a few college-level courses so I had a sense of what to expect. The program demystified the whole idea of college: it helped me to see that this was something within reach, something that I could do, should do, and was expected to do. It was an investment in my ability to be a contributing member of society, and I've spent my whole life trying to make good on that investment.

<center>✦</center>

Starting at Morehouse, I met and worked with a series of Black male mentors who came to define my approach to the ministry and to the community.

My formal mentorship into the ministry was set in motion by Reverend Lawrence Edward Carter Sr. Dean Carter, as we called him, is the dean of the Martin Luther King Jr. Chapel at Morehouse, where he has run the Chapel Assistants Program since 1979. As he has with so many young men, Dean Carter exposed me to the intellectual traditions of Christianity and the practical aspects of the ministry. He doesn't get nearly the credit he deserves, but he has single-handedly mentored many young Black men who are now pastors in some of the most influential pulpits in our country.

Dean Carter was also responsible for introducing me to another Black man who had a tremendous influence on my life: the Rev. Dr. John Thomas Porter. Dr. Porter was the pastor of the Sixth Avenue Baptist Church in Birmingham, Alabama. He had been Martin Luther King Jr.'s pulpit assistant as a young man. I interned for Dr. Porter in the summers of '90 and '91, and that's when I became a Baptist—he licensed me, ordained me in the Baptist Church, and gave me my first real shot at ministry. He embodied for me what it means to be the pastor, not only of your church, but of an entire city.

As I returned to Morehouse for my senior year, I was still $7,000 short on tuition even after my grants and loans—I'll never forget that Dr. Porter's church made a further investment in me by covering that $7,000.

Later, when I studied at Union Seminary in New York in the early 1990s, I had the good fortune to work at Abyssinian under the leadership of the Rev. Dr. Calvin Butts. Dr. Butts was also a community servant as much as a church servant. He engaged in social and political activism. He mobilized people around the Central Park jogger case, and he was a force

to be reckoned with on big issues like the preponderance of alcohol and tobacco advertising in Black communities. He led a campaign that literally went through the community whitewashing billboards. Politicians seeking elective office knew that Dr. Butts's endorsement and support were vital to their success.

Finally, at Union I was also mentored by James Cone, the father of Black Liberation Theology. Professor Cone was my advisor and was instrumental in expanding my intellectual horizons. I had been good academically, but Professor Cone inspired me to be an academic. I completed my PhD under his tutelage. That was a critical and final piece to the tripartite model that has governed my work ever since: pastor, activist, and scholar.

✦

As the senior pastor at Ebenezer Baptist Church, I've tried to be a good citizen, a good leader, and a servant to the whole community. My work has been at the intersection of the church, the academy, and the needs of ordinary people in their communities—what I call "connecting the ivory towers to the ebony trenches."

One of the issues that I've addressed, not just in my preaching but in my activism, is mass incarceration and the profound inequities in the criminal justice system. America represents 5 percent of the world's population, but we house 25 percent of the world's prisoners. America imprisons a greater share of its Black population than did South Africa at the height of apartheid.

This is the glaring moral contradiction of our time. Like segregation and lynchings during the era of Jim Crow, it is a tragic descendant of America's continuing racial past and a central moral issue for the current era. It is the issue that future gener-

ations will look back on and ask church leaders and citizens in general why we didn't do more to address it.

I have been involved in cases that exhibit the inequities in our system—for instance, the case of Genarlow Wilson. Genarlow was a B+ student and an athlete in Douglasville, Georgia. When he was seventeen, he was sentenced to ten years in prison for having oral sex with a fifteen-year-old at a wild party he and some other teenagers were having in a hotel room.

The kid clearly made a mistake, but he became ensnared by a Georgia state law that was not intended for him. The spirit of the law was good—"We're not going to tolerate adult sexual predators of children." But everybody agreed that the law was intended to catch adults preying on children, not children engaged in adolescent behavior—behavior that we all deplore, but that parents of teenagers can nevertheless relate to. In fact, the legislature agreed so much that they went back and passed the Romeo and Juliet provision of the law that would have prevented Genarlow from doing the extensive prison time that he did.

However, the law was not applied retroactively, and Genarlow remained in prison.

I got involved with Genarlow Wilson and his case. I became a pastor to and supporter of his family. I joined other community leaders in speaking out for him, including Jimmy Carter. The case finally went to the Georgia Supreme Court, and Genarlow was ultimately released from prison after nearly three years.

I saw that Genarlow was a smart kid, who matured in wisdom and in spirit throughout the whole experience. After he left prison, I called the then president of Morehouse College, Dr. Robert Michael Franklin, and encouraged him to admit Genarlow, assuming he met the requirements. Ultimately, Tom Joyner ended up giving him a scholarship and he attended

Morehouse. He graduated two years ago and now he's married with a child. He's doing fine.

✦

Over the last three years, I've been leading a project to move Ebenezer Baptist to a higher place in terms of community engagement, in bridging the ivory towers with the ebony trenches.

At the height of the recession we built a community center named in honor of Martin Luther King Sr., whom many affectionately called "Daddy King." The community center houses four nonprofit organizations: Operation Hope, which is focused on financial literacy; the Casey Family Programs, focused on reducing the number of kids in foster care and improving foster care; the Center for Working Families, which focuses on getting the chronically unemployed back to work; and the Nasro Foundation, which helps young people who've aged out of foster care to get to, and through, college. We are working to create a one-stop shop for community transformation and personal development.

✦

I have done my best to do what my mentor Dr. Porter did in Birmingham and what Dr. King did on a massive scale: be a pastor not just to my church, but to the entire city and community. I believe this is part and parcel of the calling to the pulpit. It's not just about the pastoring—it's about the activism, the scholarship, the genuine commitment to linking the ivory towers to the ebony trenches. At the end of the day, it's about genuinely advancing our human rights and our collective human potential.

Commander Paul Tanks

AGE: 51

TITLE: US Navy (Ret.); Senior Naval Science Instructor, Monterey High School NJROTC

COMMUNITY: Monterey, CA

When I was five years old I was taken away from my mom, all because of something I said.

I was born in 1963 in Harlem, the oldest of six. My early childhood was not all that great. Harlem was a rough neighborhood at the time, and it seemed like everyone that I knew in my family was suffering from a drug problem, from my mother, my father, who died when I was two, to my uncle and eventually my brothers.

When I was five years old I was living in an abandoned building with my mom, brothers, and other addicts. It was pretty much a shooting gallery. One night I was outside of the building at one or two in the morning, waiting for my mom to come back, and this white police officer came by, walking his beat. He asked what I was doing outside, and I told him I was waiting for my mom. He asked where I lived and I pointed to

the building. A shady look came over his face, and he called for backup and put me in the police car. The police raided the building and arrested pretty much everyone in it, including my mom.

I was sent to live in a Catholic orphanage before moving in with my grandmother in the Bronx. For a long time I felt that if I hadn't said anything, I wouldn't have been separated from my mom.

When I moved to the Bronx, I started going to school regularly for the first time. I was already far behind in reading and other subjects, and it was a struggle. Then when I was nine I met Mrs. Palmer. She was my fourth-grade teacher, and she turned my life around.

I remember I was just starting to get in trouble—it was easier to skip school or be defiant in class rather than suffer the embarrassment from a wrong answer or, even worse, from being asked to read out loud. But Mrs. Palmer sat me down and asked me, "Boy, what do you want to do?" Like any other kid I said, "Oh, I want to play basketball." And she told me, "I've seen you play basketball, and you're not that good."

That shook me. She pressed me for another answer, so I told her what I really wanted to do—I wanted to fly planes. I never believed that I would actually be able to do it—I didn't think I was smart enough. But to my surprise, she didn't laugh at me. She said, "Okay, prove it. You see that building over there? That's a library. Go into that library and read everything you can put your hands on about flying. Otherwise everything you're saying is a lot of bull."

Just to get out of her face I told her I would, and eventually I did walk into the library, and I picked up the first book on flying that I saw. It was the autobiography of Eddie Ricken-backer, who was the highest-scoring American ace in World War I. I read the book—it was long for someone my age, over

four hundred pages—and after that everything started to fall into place.

✦

I fell for aviation and the military hook, line, and sinker. When it was time for high school, I applied to Aviation High School in Long Island City. As a fourteen-year-old I joined the Civil Air Patrol, which is an auxiliary of the air force. They do rescue missions, that kind of stuff. It was exactly what I needed.

I had never had any male figures around. I needed someone to keep me disciplined and help me stay focused. And that's what I got from the Civil Air Patrol. We would do marches and drills—left, right, that kind of thing. I joined a team called the Bronx Group Drill Team. I was just getting to the age when I was starting to get a little wild, where a female could get me out of control. But I had senior members of the Civil Air Patrol who were on my case, making sure I did my schoolwork and came to practice. I learned so much from these two organizations, lessons that I value to this day.

I ended up graduating from the New York Institute of Technology and was selected to Aviation Officer Candidate School. I was commissioned as an ensign in the US Navy and was assigned flight training as a naval flight officer. I was finally getting the chance to fly. I successfully earned my wings and was assigned to fly the S-3B Viking and deployed aboard the aircraft carrier USS *Saratoga*. I deployed numerous times to the Mediterranean, the Middle East, and the Pacific. During my career I served in numerous jobs, from public affairs officer to flight instructor, eventually obtaining the rank of commander with twenty-one years of military service.

In 2007, the plane that I originally flew, the S-3B, was already retired, and the prospect of learning to fly a new aircraft was slim to none. I took it as a sign that it was time to get out.

Right around this time I was stationed in Corpus Christi, Texas, and someone put a pamphlet on my desk that talked about Navy Junior ROTC (NJROTC). I looked at it and thought this might be good to do for a while to give something back. I was thinking of Mrs. Palmer, who had taken time for me.

Originally, I was only going to do the Navy Junior ROTC for only one year. But it ended up changing my life.

◆

Today I'm the senior naval science instructor for Monterey High School NJROTC in California. The goal of NJROTC is to produce more informed citizens and teach kids about leadership, self-esteem, and naval science. Eighty to 90 percent of students in the program have no interest in going into the military and probably never will. But they all gain something from the program.

Just like I did as a kid, the students flock to the structure—to the discipline, the family-like environment. I make them march, but the marching itself is not important—who cares how well a kid can march? The marching is just a tool to help them learn about themselves.

About half the kids at Monterey High are Hispanic and about 9 percent are Black, and a significant amount come from low income communities. I know from experience that when you come from an environment where you don't have any real discipline, where your parents are dealing with their own issues, you are looking for that sense of security.

I try to push the kids out of their comfort zones. For instance, if I have someone who's very shy and stays in the back, I'll put them in a leadership position where they have to be out in front. For someone who's really outgoing, I'll put them in a position where they have to follow the shy person and help them out. It's about giving them an opportunity to

identify their strengths and weaknesses and work on developing them.

My first year here, I didn't know what the heck I was doing. You really have to learn how to be a mentor. At the end of the year, one of my students, Alma, I think she was seventeen, came to me and told me that her family was moving to San Diego. She would be transferring out of school. I told her that was too bad, because I was looking forward to watching her walk across the football field for graduation. She started crying. I thought, "Oh my God, here I go, I just made this teenage girl cry." But when she calmed down she told me why she was crying. She said, "You're the only one that made me feel that I could graduate."

That's when I realized how much power my words could have on the students' lives. Alma was the reason I decided to stay on at Monterey for another year, and I've been here for seven years.

✦

When I first started my job, I was surprised to learn that there were only two Black male teachers in the whole school district. I think a lot of that has to do with our definition of success.

Growing up, being a high school teacher was the last thing on my mind. My ego was telling me "I have an engineering degree, I should be doing something big." The last thing I was thinking about was doing something for my community. If anything, I wanted to get out of my community. I think that's a common theme with a lot of Black men and women. But while you're striving, you risk turning your back on the people that need you.

Part of what has helped me understand this has been my experience with a program here in Monterey called the Breakthrough Men's Community. The program is a resource for men

to step back, take a pause, and reconsider the "rules" they have set for themselves since adolescence. In my case, I discovered that my desire to emerge unscathed from the trauma of childhood led me to develop a striving, hard-charging attitude. I was set on achieving, on gaining success. It was useful, but as an adult and as a teacher I've found it useful to let part of that go and focus on the heart.

My goal right now is to make sure that all the students in my classes graduate and go on to college. A lot of them will be first-generation college students. I try to make all of them feel that they are capable of going to college. And I give them the example of myself. I didn't think I was smart enough to go to college, but I was pushed to try by ordinary people who simply took time to help me believe in myself.

I've learned that no matter what level of success you've achieved or haven't achieved, everyone has a story that could touch a kid in ways that you have no way of knowing until you experience it. Just by being who you are, just by taking the time, you can motivate someone. It can really be surprising.

Lamman Rucker

AGE: 43

TITLE: Actor; Activist; Educator;
Entrepreneur

COMMUNITY: Pittsburgh, PA;
Washington, DC; the Caribbean

I think it's natural for the creative spirit to identify something that's unjust and to resist it. Artists have a vehicle and a voice to speak out against injustice, and I think that because we have that vehicle and the gift of creative expression, we have a responsibility to do so.

I mean, imagine a civil rights movement with no music! Imagine marches without chants and the energy of the call-and-response! It's impossible to imagine. Artistic expression and activism go hand in hand.

✦

My parents were artist-scholar Black revolutionaries in the 1970s. My mother is a beautiful dancer, choreographer, and poet. There is an awesome photo of my mother visibly pregnant with me while dancing. My father is a powerful master African

drummer who also makes instruments. As a kid, I helped him skin the hair from cowhides and sand down drum barrels to make traditional African drums. So you can only imagine the dynamic and passionate energy between those two: a drummer and a dancer. Fire! That's where I come from.

I remember my parents living life kind of like Gypsies when I was very young. I could be wrong, but my early memories up until I was four or so are of us always moving, living with other family members, or traveling with other people. I can think of four or five different addresses before starting first grade. My parents seemed to take me everywhere. I was taking in the world literally from my mother's back, wrapped tight in African material, and hoisted up high. I always remember lots of people around, too—familiar faces and new ones.

Once my dad joined the navy in the eighties, we moved around even more—maybe four times between the fifth and ninth grades—including to Japan. Wherever we went, even though we might be included in the military population, my parents always made sure we were also part of an artistic community. Immersed in the local culture, we basked in the arts, theater, music, poetry, visual art, performance art, language, and history around us. My parents always surrounded themselves with very positive, dynamic, intelligent, conscious, and progressive people, too.

Some of my fondest memories from childhood come from the years we lived in Pittsburgh, though, where a community of artists formed a dance and performing arts company called the Pittsburgh Black Theater Dance Ensemble, of which my parents were members. Any musician, writer, choreographer, or performer from that era with Pittsburgh roots that you can think of crossed our paths or was a family friend—Geri Allen, George Benson, August Wilson, Abu Jamal, Otis Salid, Phyllis Hyman, and there were more.

It became a beautiful "African village" of creative, academic, and politically active people. All of us babies and children who were raised in this rich environment call each other cousins and call one another's parents aunts and uncles to this very day.

Many in the dance company may have also been doing their own thing individually but contributed their talents to what was being developed collectively. It was powerful. There was an incredible feeling of activism and social responsibility flowing through the company and the greater artistic community. It was particularly amazing to see manhood, fatherhood, and brotherhood modeled in an inspiring way. They were good people, conscientious people who did their best to do good and give back.

I followed this example and stayed involved in community after I moved to Washington, DC, and attended high school at the Duke Ellington School of the Arts. Only fourteen years old at this point, I decided to combine my interests in mentoring and theater by volunteering at Planned Parenthood in a program called W.A.I.T.T.: the Washington Area Improvisational Teen Theater.

W.A.I.T.T.'s goal was to encourage abstinence (hence the acronym "Wait") and to educate young people about sex and sexual health at a time when DC was suffering from high rates of teen pregnancy, gun violence, and people contracting HIV and dying of AIDS.

Once we received our certification as peer educators, the members of our troupe taught kids about sex and sexual health the best way we knew how—through our artistry. We created a live show that we took to schools where we performed songs, dance, poetry, rap, and improvised skits focusing on our message and other issues affecting young people.

I created and performed a fictional monologue about teen fatherhood. I was always hearing about what it was like to be a

teenage mother, but nobody was speaking to or for young men or boys who found themselves with a child. If anything, there was a stigma around these guys, an assumption that they were always running away from responsibility.

My monologue was from the perspective of a young father who was saying, "I'm here. I'm sixteen. I don't know what I'm doing, but I'm trying." I would talk about the experience of sex itself—"I didn't really know what I was doing, but I didn't stop because I didn't want her to know that I didn't know." I tried to show young men that it's okay to not be Mr. Sexual Prowess. That's not what makes you a man.

These were the Reagan/Bush years, so there were frequent anti-abortion protesters outside Planned Parenthood holding signs and shouting at anyone who came in or out. It was tense at times. Our training sessions were canceled a couple of times because protesters made bomb threats.

Nevertheless, I think our group had a lot of success in encouraging young people that you don't need to be sexually active yet, and in teaching them the facts about how their bodies work, about STDs and HIV/AIDS. There were some fifth graders who had no clue what we were talking about, and yet there were fourth graders who knew exactly what we were talking about. Every day after a show another kid would come up to us crying or sharing with us something personal. We would get questions from young kids that would blow your mind. We could reach them in a way that their teachers and parents couldn't.

✦

In 2007, a few fellow actors, writers, and directors and I started our own theater ensemble called the Black Gents of Hollywood. Now we're expanding, so we go simply by the Black Gents.

The Black Gents' mission is to "educate, entertain, and

empower" through the arts and sciences, youth mentoring, community outreach, and sharing positive Black male images. We organized because we felt compelled to redefine, restore, and reclaim the legacy of excellence, sophistication, service, fatherhood, manhood, brotherhood, honor, and pride that should be associated with men of color. We wanted to "change the paradigm" and eradicate the negativity associated with Black men and boys.

We sponsor a wide range of activities including acting workshops, mentoring programs, speaking engagements, arts education, and job opportunities, but the foundation of our work, as always, is in our artistry.

From 2006 to 2009, the Black Gents performed and produced a piece entitled *WeBeIMe*—as in "We, Be, I, Me." I remember the first time reading the script, we were all intimidated by it, but when we got onstage and started to really delve into what it was about, we realized it was going to be powerful.

The play is a "choreopoem"-style piece. It includes eight men, who you come to find out are all actually one man. Each of us onstage represents that man at a different time in his life. You learn that he's on death row, getting ready to be executed. Over the course of the play, you discover that he's lived in a cycle of neglect and abuse that led to him lashing out in a moment of impulsive violence. Most violence comes from a place of pain. The emotional pain he experienced in the moment before his impulsive reaction stems from a combination of things: his immaturity, the death of his mother when he was a child, his inability to express his feelings, the love of his life moving away, etc.

The play is a symbolic look at a microcosm of a Black man's life. It looks at mechanisms and obstacles that hold us back, provoke us, discourage us, emasculate us, or oppress us. But at the same time, the play has many moments that expose our

magnificence. It's really about the power of the human spirit to transform beyond victimhood and do phenomenal things if we are resilient. Self-destruction is a choice. We must take responsibility for our choices yet know that there are things in the world we cannot change. What we do control is our response to what happens to us.

It's a profound story, and it's become a vehicle for a dialogue around domestic violence and sexual violence toward men and boys. Just like the work I did with W.A.I.T.T. and Planned Parenthood helped adults and other young people to understand teenagers, WeBeIMe has been able to enlighten and liberate people, and expand their understanding about what it means to be a Black man: our feelings, our fears, our needs, our potential, our joys, and our aspirations.

✦

No matter what culture, no matter what time period, it's often been the artists who spark revolution or society's evolution. They won't pick up a gun, sword, or spear, but they will document the injustice, provide the commentary, and challenge the status quo. They can hide the weaponry within their artistry.

I've always been taught, from childhood, that our job as men is to lift our children up higher than ourselves. I've tried to live my life and give back in a way that leads other people to invest and believe in our young Black boys as much as they believe in boys of any color. Underneath my name is "Actor; Activist; Educator; Entrepreneur." Putting all these traits and identities together has been a challenge throughout my life, but they have begun to merge seamlessly over the last several years. Living up to these titles is work. I see it as more than just a responsibility to serve in so many ways—it's an awesome adventure and an incredible privilege.

Derrick Johnson

AGE: 46

TITLE: State President, Mississippi NAACP; Executive Director, One Voice

COMMUNITY: Mississippi

My role models growing up were black men that I called my uncles—though three of them were not blood relatives. My uncles took care of me, and in a way I took care of them in return.

My mother raised me alone in inner-city Detroit. The previous generation of my family had migrated to Detroit from the South in order to get good jobs in the auto industry, but after Reaganomics and the decline of the unions, those jobs went away. By the early 1980s, when I was coming up, it was drugs and poverty all around.

My uncles all lived in the neighborhood, and they were all veterans of World War II and the Korean War. They were black men who eked out existences as handymen, laborers at the car wash, garbagemen, and carpenters—blue collar men.

There was Uncle DC, who was the husband of one of my great-aunts. He was illiterate and he didn't drive, but he was an

archetype of honor and conscientiousness. He visited us every Saturday morning for breakfast, and he could tell these vivid stories. Since he didn't drive, I started taking him to work when I got my license.

There was Uncle Jimmy, who lived next door to us. He was a garbage collector for the city. Jimmy knew the Bible front and back and could quote Scriptures. He always reminded me to keep an even temper in life. He was fond of citing the biblical story of Zachariah, who got up too high—forgot to be humble—and fell off the tree. He was also an alcoholic, so when he came home from work on Fridays I helped him make sure he didn't lose his paycheck.

There was also Adele, who was always happy to pick me up if I was stranded and needed to get home, and Lee, who was like my stepfather, even though he and my mom never got married.

I was the poor little rich kid on the block. If I ever needed something—clothes, travel, anything—my uncles made sure I had it.

✦

After high school I bounced around a few colleges before landing at Mary Holmes College in Mississippi. Mary Holmes was where I began my education about the civil rights movement.

At Mary Holmes my literature professor, Dr. Simmons, assigned us *The Fire Next Time*, by James Baldwin. Baldwin's account captured some of my realities in Detroit growing up in the church. Outside the church doors there was chaos with the drugs and with the whole culture. Inside the church, there was a sense of peace and promise. I would sit in the library during my work-study job, mesmerized by the book.

One of the librarians, Ms. Parkman, noticed my fascination, and when I finished the book she slid another book in front of me: *Assata: An Autobiography*, by Assata Shakur. After that, the li-

brarian fed me a steady stream of books about Medgar Evers and the history of the NAACP in Mississippi. I learned about civil rights heroes like CC Bryant, Bob Moses, and so many others.

✦

I also learned about Dr. Aaron Henry, who had been a friend and collaborator of Medgar Evers and at the time was the state president of the Mississippi NAACP. As it happened, Dr. Henry's daughter attended Mary Holmes at the same time I did, and she was a dorm counselor.

One night my friend and I got caught sneaking into the women's dorms at Mary Holmes after hours. Sneaking into the dorms was a serious offense, and we could have been suspended from living on campus. We were caught, and we were sent to Dr. Henry's daughter for punishment.

When we met her we pleaded our case, begging her not to suspend us. She agreed to give us a second chance, but she said she thought we needed to channel our energy more effectively. She told me, "Why don't you start a campus chapter of the NAACP? My father is the state conference president—bring the students and we'll help you."

There was not an NAACP chapter on campus, so we chartered one. Within three weeks, we got sixty students to join and pay dues. There was a convenience store that would not serve black customers—this was 1990—so we organized a demonstration against them.

Soon afterward, Dr. Henry's daughter invited us to the NAACP State Conference in Louisville, Mississippi. Her father picked us up and drove us to Louisville. I was in shock. Here I was, riding in a car with someone I'd been reading about in what I thought were history books.

We got to the meeting and I realized that the people I saw around me were the people I had been reading about—I

thought they were figures of history, but they were still very active, and the work they were doing was still relevant. The education chair was proposing a boycott of a local school district, and one of the NAACP's lawyers was preparing to argue a case in front of the Supreme Court. I was hooked.

In 1991, I graduated from the two-year program at Mary Holmes. Ms. Parkman, the librarian, encouraged me to transfer to Tougaloo College in Jackson, Mississippi. Tougaloo is an HBCU (Historically Black College and University) with a remarkable intellectual and political history. Just a few years earlier, members of the African National Congress (ANC) and the Pan Africanist Congress (PAC) had visited during the height of apartheid. The sense of Afrocentricity and collective action was palpable.

I quickly joined the NAACP campus chapter and helped grow it from 27 to 138 students in a matter of weeks. I was eventually elected president of the chapter as well as youth president of the Mississippi NAACP. We created an African Liberation Weekend and brought in speakers like Tupac Shakur. We organized demonstrations to protest the state's proposed merger of two public historically black colleges, Alcorn and Mississippi Valley State. That's where I met Hollis Watkins.

Hollis had been the first organizer for the Student Nonviolent Coordinating Committee (SNCC) in Mississippi. He became a mentor. He helped our campus chapter improve our organizing abilities. Over the next two years we were able to build our campaign in support of the HBCUs, eventually organizing a protest with fifteen thousand students. The schools remained independent and fully funded.

✦

Today I'm the executive director of One Voice, an organization I founded to train and connect community leaders in Missis-

sippi and Louisiana. Through all of our work, we are seeking to build a progressive infrastructure in the South. We host an annual leadership summit that brings together elected officials, primarily black leaders, from across Mississippi. The goal is to create a network so they can collaborate and share best practices. The hope is that it will help our leaders develop proactive solutions to some of the state's pressing problems.

We've also created a number of leadership programs to train the next generation of leaders. One program, with Congressman Bennie Thompson, teaches college students about the legislative process. Another program connects Tougaloo undergraduates with Harvard Law School students who come down South for their holiday break. We've found that the students from the two schools stay in touch with each other, and have a lot to teach each other.

Growing up where I did and the way that I did gave me a vantage point on social issues, but it also forged my values.

The first thing I learned was that no one should be discarded. No one should be left to waste away. The four gentlemen in my early life brought this into full focus. An outsider looking in would look at my Uncle DC as someone who could not read, someone who walked everywhere, and they might think he was a bum walking the street. Others would look at Jimmy and say, "He's just a garbageman and an alcoholic."

But I knew these men. They were smart and honorable. They risked their lives to fight for our country, and they only wanted to come back and be treated with dignity.

Throughout my whole career, I've been keen to treat people with dignity and respect and ensure that those of us who are the least well off have a voice. I look at individuals who work hard every day, and I believe they should be treated with the same level of respect and dignity as anyone else, if not more. They are my family.

George Gresham

AGE: 59

TITLE: President, SEIU 1199

COMMUNITY: New York, NY

For much of my childhood I lived with my grandparents. I was born in Virginia in 1955, and when I was eight years old my parents moved to New York to make a living as in-home domestic workers for a wealthy furrier on Long Island.

When my parents came down to visit I would spend all night long on the porch waiting for their car to come in, and I would cry the moment they got in the car to go back to New York. But in those in-between times, I never felt cheated.

My paternal grandfather was a truck driver, so he would be on the road every week. But on weekends he would come home, and he would pull me and my sister and cousins aside and sit with us under a big persimmon tree on our property. He would tell me the same thing every Saturday—I was going to do something to change this world, and I was destined to be a miracle child.

Virginia at the time was still segregated. If we went to the theater, we would have to sit in the balcony. If we went to buy a sandwich from the Rexall Drug Store, it was wrapped to take out. Even so, there was a code in the black community that everyone was everyone else's child.

I was disciplined and protected. If someone saw me in public misbehaving, then that person had permission to correct me and then tell my grandmother, which meant that I would get corrected again. I was able to get an education. My first school was a converted three-room house that held five grades—in two of the three rooms there was only one teacher handling two grades. But when I eventually moved to New York with my parents and attended my first integrated school—in Harlem, of all places—I tested ahead of the other students my age and was able to skip a grade. The education I got in the segregated school in Virginia was more advanced than the education kids were getting in New York.

✦

In New York, the biggest thing I had to adjust to was not speaking to every black person that I saw. Because in the South, that's what you do. No matter where you are, you speak to each other. In New York, people would look at me weird. My mother had to keep reminding me, everyone is an individual up here.

I arrived in New York at a time when the Black Panthers and the Young Lords were active. There was great change going on in the country, and people of color, particularly black people, were standing up for their rights.

I was attracted to those organizations, and it worried my father. He was a leftist, but he didn't want me joining an organization where I could easily be killed by a police officer. He reminded me that real power is in the collective. When you

narrow yourself to one particular category—in my case black nationalism—you narrow your movement.

A big turning point in my family's life was when my father became a Teamster. Not only did our lives improve about 3,000 percent, but we saw firsthand the power of collective strength. Back then, nobody messed with the Teamsters when they united. They were able to make real change. I started to understand my father's lesson about the power of the collective.

✦

When I was recently out of high school I got a job at Presbyterian Hospital, in the housekeeping department, and I joined the union, SEIU 1199. I worked for three years in housekeeping before earning some seniority, and I was offered an upgrade as a clerk typist in the neural radiological department.

I still remember the first day that I arrived at the radiological department. I looked around and I saw that out of forty-five people in the department, it was nearly all white, with the exception of one person. This was the midseventies, and at the time I had a fairly large-size Afro and an earring in one ear. I went to the supervisor, a white lady who was so fascinated by my earring that she couldn't look me in the eye—her eyes were on my ear the whole time. She told me that the director of the department, Dr. Hilal, was on vacation for three weeks, and that no one got hired without his approval. I would have to wait.

At that point, my experience in the South was starting to affect my confidence. I told myself, there's no way I'm going to get this job. I would be without a job for three weeks, and then when Dr. Hilal got back, there was no way he would hire my black ass.

I went back to the personnel office and told them about the conversation. To my surprise, management picked up

the phone right away and called the supervisor. She told her, "Josephine, you may have forgotten that there is a union here now, and Dr. Hilal does not have a choice on who he hires. Mr. Gresham fits the qualifications, so I expect him to start."

I was so impressed. Everything that I had seen in life basically told me that I was going to get discriminated against. But just by mentioning the union, I was able to get the job. I became very active in the union after that.

✦

One of my greatest frustrations is when I see people who have made it, and the more they make it, the more it becomes about them. As if they were born to have success; as if there weren't circumstances and luck that paved the way for them to have that opportunity. That's so disappointing, because that attitude is not going to keep our community strong as a unit.

A lot of folks in our organization say that had it not been for 1199, they would have ended up in jail or dead. We literally take care of our members and their children from cradle to grave. We have summer camps, youth mentoring programs, scholarships—they may not be large scholarships, but they help.

We've learned that not everybody is attracted by the militant fear of the union. You've got to let people see the other side of the union, the community-building side, and those people often become some of our strongest members. It's simply good organizing.

Just recently we completed negotiations on a major contract. We finished up at 4:30 A.M., and many of our members stayed up with our leadership as we ironed out the details. There were a number of times during the process when management tried to divide the workers by category, so that different workers would receive different benefits and different pay scales. But

when they tried to do that there were five hundred people in the room shouting, "One union, one union!"

It wasn't even choreographed. Management didn't believe that, but I told them—we didn't practice this.

You need that sense of collective power when you are dealing with workers who are often not highly skilled and who are majority people of color, majority women. The union creates a real sense of pride—a sense that there is dignity in our work, no matter what we do.

I'm proud to be part of an organization that has a strong track record of building successful movements. I like to think that I'm helping build the sense of community that was so common in segregated Virginia when I was a child, and is too often missing in New York today. Our members understand that individually we may not be strong, but collectively, we can change things.

Stephen DeBerry

AGE: 40

TITLE: Social Impact Investor

COMMUNITY: East Palo Alto and Mill Valley, CA

Few know this about me, but I am willing to confess that I am a bit of a conspiracy theorist. I arrived at this view through one of my favorite books, *The Alchemist*. A central theme of the book is that when any of us pursues our truest passion the universe will conspire with us to help us achieve our goal. I'm enamored with this idea. I believe it. I also believe that even with the awesome tailwind of the universe at our backs there are still a few things we have to do to ensure we reach our goals. I'd like to talk about those things here: toil, discovery, and acceptance.

I could have easily used the word "work" instead of toil, but to do so would discount the brute reality that to achieve the most coveted things folks invariably have to toil away at a level that only makes sense for someone genuinely pursuing his or her deepest passion. I'm reminded that after painting the Sistine Chapel Michelangelo said, "If people knew how hard

I had to work to gain my mastery, it would not seem so wonderful at all." I also think of another craftsman who was no less masterful—my grandmother—whose neighbor commented on her consistently full and proud rosebushes by saying, "Laura, your flowers are always so glorious. You really do have a green thumb." My grandmother shot back, "I don't have a green thumb. I have a workin' ass!" The universe only conspires with those who are willing to trade toil for the gift of accomplishment, whatever the endeavor.

The point of discovery is that the path to realizing our passion may end up looking entirely different from what we expect. Therefore, we must explore new things and remain open to shifting circumstances while keeping our eyes on the essential nature of the prize, as opposed to how the prize is delivered. Did you know that before Whoopi Goldberg built her screen presence she was a makeup artist at a mortuary? Not everyone will have such a radical transition, but being open to discovery and having openness to entirely new paths increase the chance of realizing a dream because they create more possible paths to get there.

Finally, acceptance is about truly believing you can achieve your greatest desire—owning it—and then allowing others to help you get there. We can be misled by the myth of individual success, but the reality is that along the way to each success there is usually at least one key actor who enabled that success. The universe can't conspire with you if you don't let it. Being able to accept help is a sign of strength, not weakness.

✦

I am forty years old now, and after looking back at the arc of my life thus far I realize this theme of the universe conspiring has held true through my endeavors in several areas—from athletics to education to business.

My life as an athlete has spanned from being a high school football player, to being a national champion track athlete, to adopting new and challenging sports like high-altitude mountain climbing, in which I was part of the first all-African-American expedition to climb Denali, the highest peak in North America. With each evolution I learned to incorporate toil, discovery, and acceptance to my benefit.

Floyd Mayweather Jr., the champion boxer, is a complex personality to many people, but one thing I absolutely love about him is his training mantra that "all work is easy work." That's the toil mind-set of a champion. I was involuntarily introduced to that mind-set in "two a day" practices in high school football, where I experienced the counterintuitive reality that piling more work on can make the work you have easier. That is an invaluable lesson.

My goal as a high school football player was to get a scholarship to go to college. The reality was that I was a very good player, but not world-class. I learned to focus on what made me distinct, and at 165 pounds it surely wasn't my size. However, I was faster and more nimble than most, so as a sophomore I explored track and field. I discovered that I did have a chance to be world-class running hurdles. By keeping my eyes on the ultimate goal of getting a scholarship, as opposed to being fixated on football per se, I increased the number of ways I could succeed. I ended up with offers to play football in college but after becoming the national champion in the 400-meter hurdles I accepted a track scholarship to UCLA.

The hard work was mine to do, but getting that track scholarship was only possible due to the help I had. I came home in between our morning and evening two-a-day football practices my senior year in high school to find my father, a US Marine, packing gear for his deployment to the first Gulf War. While he was irreplaceable, I was fortunate to have my coach, Bill

Wilhite, as a surrogate supporter. Coach Wilhite prodded me forward and helped me identify my niche as a hurdler. He is one of countless examples of African-American men stepping up to support each other. Without him I never would have made it to UCLA.

✦

The universe also conspired when it came to my education. I went from failing algebra in high school to graduating with highest honors from UCLA and ultimately being selected as a Marshall Scholar and receiving two graduate degrees from the University of Oxford in England. Along the way there was plenty of toil, discovery, and acceptance.

I played on my high school basketball team, which meant I often missed my sixth-period algebra class for game travel. When I'd return, I'd often ask for an explanation of what I missed, which frustrated my teacher, so much so she ultimately told me she hated me. That devastated me. I stopped asking questions because I didn't want to feel hated. As a result, I lost critical building blocks and ultimately figured I was just no good at math. I failed algebra that term, despite being class president and doing well in the rest of my course work. It wasn't until I got to UCLA and started statistics with a clean slate that I challenged myself to toil methodically through each step of the work, sometimes taking hours per night, but getting an A+ in that class and regaining my confidence about my quantitative abilities. I'm a financial investor now, and needless to say, I'm quite comfortable with math.

My goal in college was to reach my highest potential as a person, which at the time seemed like making it to the Olympics as a hurdler. However, I broke my hip in a race my freshman year, so that dream was deferred. I didn't walk for two months. That term I took an anthropology class, basically

because a girl I liked was taking it and I wanted an excuse to sit by her. I quickly realized that anthropology was way more interesting than the girl, and I met the coolest professor I could imagine. Professor Marcy Morgan researched hip-hop culture. By being open to discovering anthropology I found the freedom to pursue my natural curiosity about hip-hop and popular culture in an academically rigorous way.

My parents always taught me that I could choose to do anything at all. What mattered was that I be the best at whatever I chose to do. My Olympic aspirations were built along those lines, but after discovering a love for a more academic path I needed a new role model. Bill Clinton was the president at the time, and he was a Rhodes Scholar, so I figured why not shoot for that? It took some time but I mustered the audacity to accept the possibility that I could achieve a similar path to the president's. I wanted to go to Oxford, but the wrinkle was I wanted to write about hip-hop. Once I committed to that path Dr. Morgan and the head of UCLA's College Honors program went to bat for me with the Rhodes and Marshall Scholarship committees.

After plenty of academic toil and staying true to my love for hip-hop and anthropology, and with the help of Dr. Morgan, I was a finalist in the Rhodes selection process and ultimately won the Marshall Scholarship that paid for me to go to Oxford, just like the president. It took time to convince myself it was possible, and accepting that possibility is a major part of why I think it happened. And I did it all with hip-hop at the center, no less! That was empowering and taught me that I could succeed while being true to myself.

Finally, my life in business has had a grand design of its own. My business career has grown from selling used golf balls at age nine, to supporting tech deals and strategy for some of the seminal figures in technology, to founding my own firm

and crafting a new approach to investing. Along the way there's been plenty of toil, discovery, and acceptance.

I graduated with a master's degree in anthropology and an MBA from Oxford, where I'd been running a small Web development business from my room on campus. I had an odd skill set blending social analysis, technology, and business and didn't know where I fit in. Fortunately, a fellow Marshall Scholar alumnus suggested I talk to Paul Allen's research lab, where I might be a great fit. I didn't know who Paul Allen was at the time but quickly learned that he had cofounded Microsoft with Bill Gates. Being open to that discovery set me on a path I couldn't have imagined. Since then I've been able to work with Paul as well as Pierre Omidyar, the founder of eBay, and Mitch Kapor, founder of Lotus Development Corporation. Thank God I was open to explore these new paths.

After working with such a cast of amazing founders, I began to imagine I might be able to build something big and meaningful. I founded Bronze Investments in 2009, and it continues to be a process of both learning to accept its potential in my own mind and identifying others who fundamentally believe in using business as a force for social good who can help me. Mitch Kapor and Freada Kapor Klein were early supporters of my work, and as Bronze grows more meaningful they remain on my list of folks to give thanks to.

The single hardest thing I have done professionally was to convince an investor to commit $45 million to Bronze so I could invest in companies that make money by doing good. (This was kind of like convincing the British government to send me to Oxford so I could think about hip-hop culture— achievable, but far from obvious how.) Because I started Bronze on nights and weekends on top of my "day job," I consistently worked more than a hundred hours per week for well over a year—nonstop. Talk about toil! It was not uncommon for me

to sit at my desk in the morning and be so enthralled that the sky would darken before I'd realize I'd been sitting all day without eating or going out.

Through Bronze Investments I've helped build alternatives to predatory payday lending and even helped build a low-cost, high-quality university, among other things. This is my truest passion and I think the universe knows that. I'm so very grateful for the opportunity to keep using all of my faculties to make the world a better place.

◆

When I look back at how the idea that "the universe conspires" has played out in my life, it becomes clear that this notion isn't some mysterious or mystical conspiracy. To the contrary. The universe is comprised of all of us—everyday people—who choose to toil for our deepest passions with abandon. The universe is full of those who help guide others to discover new paths to old goals. The universe is made of each one of us who learns to believe in our own limitless potential and accept help from others to realize that potential. The universe is us—every single one of us. We are mutually interdependent, whether we acknowledge it or not. This is why we must continue to reach toward each of our greatest aspirations.

Talib Kweli Greene

AGE: 39

TITLE: Musician

COMMUNITY: Brooklyn, NY

I was grounded in activism, education, and self-love from the very beginning.

African-centered education was stressed in my household when I was growing up. My brother and I were given African names—Talib Kweli for me, and Jamal Kwame for him. We wore African-centered garb around the house, and we celebrated Kwanzaa. African art and images decorated our home. My parents did a lot to make sure that my brother and I knew that our legacy as a people extended far beyond the stereotypical images of blacks throughout the diaspora.

My parents met in 1969 at New York University, where they became involved in antiwar activism and black cultural nationalism. My father was more of a hippie type, protesting the war in Vietnam. My mother was part of the Black Student Union.

She was one of the first recipients of the King Scholarship, which was started right after Dr. King was murdered.

We lived in Park Slope, Brooklyn. In the 1970s, when I was coming up, the neighborhood wasn't as fancy as it is now. My parents were teachers and didn't make a lot of money, but our household was rich in spirit and rich in education. My mother was part of the National Organization for Women, and she and my father did antiapartheid work, as well as voter registration and political work for Roger Green, Al Vann, and other New York politicians. I can still picture all these mugs and tote bags printed with the different organizations' logos lying around the house.

In 1983, when I was six, I remember we went to Washington, DC, where there was a big protest to make Dr. King's birthday a holiday. I watched Stevie Wonder perform "Happy Birthday" on the Mall.

Then when I became a preteen, I started listening to Public Enemy and X-Clan, and I noticed that some of the messages of social justice I'd learned in my younger years had begun to reverberate throughout hip-hop.

I didn't grow up with hip-hop the way some inner-city New York kids did. My father collected vinyl records, and there was always music in our house, but he listened to just about every genre of music except hip-hop. I didn't know how to tag my name, I didn't know how to breakdance—none of that fly stuff. I was definitely an outsider.

What I did know was how to write. I wrote poetry as a child. I was eight years old when I wrote my first play. So when I would hear hip-hop lyrics, I recognized right away that they were poetry. As I listened to my favorite artists—Big Daddy Kane, Rakim, and others who were doing exceptional writing—I started to understand the power of hip-hop. By the

time I was in junior high school, I was writing songs and performing. Hip-hop had taken over my life.

◆

If you're an entertainer and you want to incorporate activism in your music, there's a choice you have to make early in your career: Do I want to put the art or the message first?

There are different schools of thought about this, and I think all of them are to be respected. There are artists who put the message first—artists like Dead Prez, Boots Riley from The Coup, or Tom Morello from Rage Against the Machine. There's nothing wrong with that, and I don't think it takes away from their particular art, but it's very clear that when you see M1 from Dead Prez out somewhere, he is representing for his movement, and the art is a vehicle for him to get his message out.

Personally, I have a different philosophy. When I'm in the studio, I choose to put the art first. Early in my career I decided that without the art, no one was going to listen to what I had to say. Even today, people don't listen to me because I'm smart or because I say fly shit—they listen to me because I'm a dope rapper. If I ever stopped being a dope rapper, people might stop wanting to listen—they might miss the message as well as the art.

Of course, outside the studio is a different story. When I'm on the ground with activists, I'm not afraid to put the message first. When I'm on TV giving an interview, I'll put the message first. When I'm telling my kids to do their homework, you better believe I put the message first. But when I'm in the studio or any other creative space, the art has got to come before anything else. That's the only way to keep it pure.

◆

The most incredible thing is when the art and the message work in tandem to change the world.

Haki R. Madhubuti said something years ago that I always remembered—that true artists provide a vision for the future. Anybody can tell you what's going on right now, but the true artist is the one who gives you a vision for what can be.

Most artists are followers. They follow the trend of what people want; they have big egos and want everyone to like them. The rare exception is the artist who sets the trend—the artist who says, "You know what? I'm going to take my plat- form and do my own thing, and I'm going to use it for some- thing good."

There are certain artists who have done that. Bob Marley took this mind-set called Rastafarianism and this unknown musical style called reggae and managed to unite the leaders of warring political parties in Jamaica—at least for a moment. Fela Kuti used Afrobeat to speak truth to power in Nigeria. Many of these artists came from places of degradation. But they were able to use their art to transcend them.

Sadly, today there aren't as many examples of artists doing the kind of work that Bob Marley and Fela did. We have artists who are popular enough to do so and be effective, but they remain disconnected from the movement.

If there was a single moment when I felt hip-hop and ac- tivism came together, it was probably in 1998, when I went to Havana, Cuba. The trip was organized by the Malcolm X Grassroots Movement; one of the things they did was to con- nect people of color and poor people and oppressed people and people who were interested in justice, raise funds for political prisoners, and generally use hip-hop as a tool for activism. It was me and my crew and Dead Prez. We went down there and met with Assata Shakur, and she told us all about her life story. I was amazed that hip-hop music had taken me to this place.

✦

People who love hip-hop often complain about it. They complain about what's on the radio; they say, "I don't hear nothing good." Sometimes I don't understand those complaints, because there are so many great artists coming up in hip-hop all the time—these artists are just not appreciated for their work on a wide scale.

I feel the same way about activism and those who criticize activists. When Michael Brown pops up, when Eric Garner pops up, when Trayvon Martin pops up, you get a lot of pushback, a lot of criticism from people who say, "Well, why are y'all going to Ferguson now? No one talks about gang violence in Chicago, or the thousands of other cases of police brutality every year." But it always turns out the pushback is coming from people who aren't doing anything themselves, who are screaming from the sidelines. They are the people who look the other way while the real activists step up every day.

I was at the protests in Ferguson, Missouri, in the weeks following the death of Michael Brown, an unarmed teenager who was shot by a police officer while his hands were raised. I talked to some of the citizens of Ferguson, the young kids—teenagers, even—at the forefront of the justice movement there. I met some people who actually quit their jobs to become full-time activists. I give it up to them.

While I was in Ferguson, I never considered myself a leader. Instead I used my status to become a resource and a voice for the people who are on the ground fighting for what's right. I helped them when I could, like offering guidance on organizing a concert. And I took direction from groups like Lost Voices, the Black Youth Project, and the Dream Defenders, people who are out there dedicating their lives to the cause.

As an activist, I know that the best way to help is to not

ignore the good work being done in places like Ferguson and across the country. Instead, I make a conscious choice to surround myself with people who are fighting for justice. I speak up on their behalf because I have the platform, and I praise their work for all to hear.

As an activist and an artist, I know there is always light at the end of the tunnel. This is why I write my music in the spirit of hope and celebration. Because if we never celebrate the victories, then why are we even fighting?

AFTERWORD

Dr. John Silvanus Wilson Jr., President, Morehouse
College

I was supposed to be an undertaker. My uncle was founder of
the Andrew W. Nix Funeral Home, a successful, growing busi-
ness in a section of Philadelphia where rampant gang activity
made morticians thrive. But three things forced me to think
about a different career path.

First, I did not like being around dead bodies. As a teen-
ager, I spent summers and some weekends working for my
uncle, and I would go into that cold and lifeless morgue . . .
and become queasy. And far too often, the bodies were those
of young black men and boys who looked like me. That made
me queasy too.

Second, as a way to cope with the creepiness of it all, I would
often try to lighten the mood with humor. So, not knowing he
was within earshot, I nearly caused my uncle to lose complete
confidence in me when his business phone rang one afternoon,
and I whimsically answered, "Nix Funeral Home, you kill 'em,
we chill 'em!" That was not exactly music to the ears of folks
calling to make funeral arrangements. Luckily, there was no

grieving family on the line. Nonetheless, while my uncle gave me a public lecture, he would later give my mother a private call to express serious doubt that I was destined to run his business.

Third, for me, these experiences engendered an abridged perspective on life. Toiling around so many broken, maimed, or dead black men made me determined that I would have nothing to do with gangs, crime, or dying young. But little did I know then that it would be hard to find success with my heart set mostly on what I did not want to be. That is where my heroic mentors surged.

My father was my hero. He was a pastor in North Philadelphia. But more than a pastor, he was what people throughout and beyond North Philly called "a preacher's preacher!" He was consistently well spoken and invariably well heard. From him, I learned the importance of discovering for myself the power of God in transcending and altering any and all earthly circumstances, no matter how bleak. And by the example of his central and unheralded role as cocreator of a pathbreaking job-training program called Opportunities Industrialization Center, or OIC, he also taught me that service to others was the true sign of a good life.

My mother was also my hero. She served as an elementary school teacher in the public school system, but she demanded far more from the four of us in her classroom at home than she ever could at work. Because we eventually moved to the white suburbs of Philadelphia, where low expectations of black kids were still the norm, she made it clear that she expected us to outperform all of the white students who surrounded us. And so we did. And then because she ensured that we joined her mother in spending many hours packing books and clothes for poor kids in Mississippi and throughout the American South, I, again, learned to aspire not toward mere leadership, but servant leadership.

I remain well aware of the advantages afforded me by such positive messages from both parents. They turned my mind and spirit toward the beauty of what I wanted to be and away from the fear of what I did not want to be. I am well aware that most young black boys, then and now, are not so blessed with two encouraging parents providing two trajectory-setting signals. But more than just giving me a personal sense of competitive advantage, that parental gift translated into a spiritual sense of compassionate obligation.

Illustrated by statistics that are all too familiar, the life outcomes for black boys are the worst for any subgroup in the nation. The only way to turn that around is if many more of us feel that same spiritual tug of compassionate obligation. And those of us who are fortunate enough to receive a competitive education are charged with the task of helping to improve the life chances of those who are not so fortunate.

I received that particular lesson from W. E. B. DuBois, who popularized the theory of the talented tenth, wherein the "best" of us must uplift the rest of us. That lesson also derives from the Bible, wherein Luke 12:48 holds, "those unto whom much is given, of them shall be much required." And for further reinforcement, that lesson came from my parents, who taught me to value such outcomes as the transformation of a black college from an old and chronic institutional condition called "needy" to a new and revitalizing institutional echelon called "nimble."

It is true that black men have been and will continue to be servant leaders. As evidenced by the many testimonies in and beyond this book, we have served as mentors, community builders, and heroes, fighting to democratize opportunities and freedoms that have benefited far too few in this country. Certainly, Morehouse College has produced a noteworthy percentage of those leaders. But we all must do more. Much more! And the most effective way to do more is to ensure that

more of us make the shift from looking to avoid death, to being determined to embrace life.

◆

I firmly believe that I am now doing what I was born to do! I encourage everyone in the springtime of living to strive for that—that is, yearn to live a call-answered life. Why? Because when you do that, you will also discover the true presence of God.

I am honored to have realized that I was not called to spend my life planning the home-going services for countless young black men. But I am also privileged to have realized that my true mission is in higher education and, more specifically, to enhance our annual production of hundreds of high-quality Morehouse men.

So, rather than becoming an undertaker, my current under-taking at Morehouse College means that my life is not about funerals but futures. And it is not about burying young black men, but elevating them, so they can build our communities like never before!

ACKNOWLEDGMENTS

Thanks to our agent, Michael Harriot, for your guidance, wisdom, and expertise. We counted on your experienced hand to guide us through the world of book publishing. Thank you to Atria and to the rest of the team at Simon & Schuster for your belief in this project and for giving these stories a home. Special thanks to Todd Hunter for your always timely support and crucial editorial direction. Thank you to Kwesi Ferebee, Nadia Khastagir, and the Design Action Collective for your ability to deliver brilliant illustrations on a tight deadline, and to Marlon Johnson, Ben Wrobel, Nicole Levey, and Kweli Washington for dedicating hours upon hours of hard work to this project. Finally, thanks to Karla Ballard, senior vice president at Participant Media, and John Seifert, chairman and CEO of Ogilvy & Mather North America, for helping us spread these stories far and wide.

And, of course, thank you to every one of the men in this book who let down their guard and opened their hearts to share their stories with us.

BEN: Thank you to my parents, my grandparents, and my sister, Lara, for teaching me how to listen with heart and speak with courage. Thank you to Mitch Kapor, Freada Kapor Klein,

Cedric Brown, Eric Wingerter, Derek Turner, and Moneese deLara—and to the rest of my colleagues at Kapor Capital and the Kapor Center for Social Impact—for understanding that genius exists in equal measure in every community, and that the future of our world depends on finding ways to unleash it for the benefit of all humanity. Thank you to the Davenport family and Jerry Lopes; to Alfred Liggins and the Radio One family; and to America's black community newspapers for lifting up the stories that matter. Thank you to the Hunt Alternatives Fund's Prime Movers program and the Center for American Progress for making this project possible. Thank you to my fellow brothers of Kappa Alpha Psi, archons of Sigma Pi Phi, and members of the NAACP for inspiring young boys and girls to reach even higher. Finally, I would like to express my gratitude to the late Charles Tisdale, Bill Lynch, and Judge Robert Watts for believing that a precocious kid with a bad stutter could make a contribution.

TRABIAN: I'd like to thank BMe's cofounders, who believe with me that together we can change the future. They are my friend Alberto Ibarguen of the Knight Foundation and my founding board members Ben Jealous of Kapor Capital, Karla Ballard of Participant Media, Stephanie Bell-Rose of TIAA-CREF, and Charles Best of Donors Choose. I'd also like to thank Team BMe, especially Sarah Bouchereau, Shaka Senghor, Benjamin Evans, Rodney Foxworth, Truman Hudson, Anthony Miller, Malcolm Sands, Jenna Buehler, and Christine Johnson, who wake up every morning thinking about how to build our beloved community—you make the movement. Thanks also to our earliest friends and allies Shawn Dove and Rashid Shabazz of the Campaign for Black Male Achievement, Tanay Allen of the Skillman Foundation, Melanie Brown of Heinz Endowment, Van Jones of Rebuild The Dream and #YesWeCode, and our entire band of Smart Optimists, as well as Jessica Johnson

of the Scholarship Academy, Dr. Phyllis Hubbard of Radiant
Health Strategies, Dr. Tyrone Bledsoe of the Student African-
American Brotherhood, and Marcus Walton, Greg Hodge, and
Susan Batten of the Association of Black Foundation Execu-
tives. I'd also like to thank Peter Bloom for helping to make this
book possible, and I'd like to acknowledge the "BMe Leaders,"
one hundred (and counting) everyday extraordinary black men
we've funded who lead by example in creating opportunities
for others. Go to http://www.bmecommunity.org to learn more
about them.

Finally, special acknowledgment to my mother, Charlene
Ellison; my inspiring brother and sister, Darwin and Shonda
Shorters; my heart, Yetunde Taiwo; my sons Marcus and Mal-
colm and their mom, Susan; my nephews Juwan and Jalen;
the whole Hutchons family; my godson, Julien; and my dear
friends Kayla Mason, Cazzy Jordan, and Kori Lane.

To learn more about

visit www.bmecommunity.org,
or follow on twitter @BMeCommunity.

To learn more about

visit www.kaporcapital.com.